T0298983

FOOD SECURITY IN AFRICA'S SECONDARY CITIES: NO. 1. MZUZU, MALAWI

LIAM RILEY, EMMANUEL CHILANGA,
LOVEMORE ZUZE, AMANDA JOYNT

SERIES EDITOR: PROF. JONATHAN CRUSH

ACKNOWLEDGEMENTS

This is the first publication in a new AFSUN series on the relationship between rapid urbanization, secondary cities, and food security in Africa. This case study of the City of Mzuzu in Malawi is funded by an Insight Grant from the Social Sciences and Humanities Research Council of Canada (SSHRC) on *Secondary Urbanization, Food Security and Local Governance in Africa*. The authors wish to thank the following for their assistance: Ruth Mbeya, Cameron McCordic, Bernard Kamanga, Yohane Nyasulu, Hannington Makamo, Agness Banda, Jowasi Banda, Maureen Chilanga, Patricia Chibwe, Trevor Gondwe, Chisomo Khanyera, Harry Kumwenda, Jason Kumwenda, Stella Mgala, Chimwemwe Mhango, Brian Mponda, Juliana Ngwira, Tabitha Niudi, Daniel Nkhoma, and Mateyo Nyirongo.

Published by the African Food Security Urban Network (AFSUN)
www.afsun.org

First published 2018

ISBN 978-1-920597-33-7

Cover photo: Ruth Mbeya (Mzuzu Market)

Production by Bronwen Dachs Muller, Cape Town

Printed by Print on Demand, Cape Town

AUTHORS

Liam Riley is a Banting Postdoctoral Fellow at the Balsillie School of International Affairs, Wilfrid Laurier University in Canada

Emmanuel Chilanga is a PhD Candidate in the Centre for Research on Children and Families, School of Social Work, McGill University, Canada, and a Lecturer of Geography at the University of Livingstonia in Malawi

Lovemore Zuze is a Lecturer in Applied Sciences: Food Security and Nutrition at the University of Livingstonia in Malawi

Amanda Joynt is a PhD Candidate in Geography and Environmental Management at the University of Waterloo in Canada

Previous Publications in the AFSUN Series

CONTENTS

TABLES

FIGURES

1. INTRODUCTION

This report marks the first stage of AFSUN's goal of expanding knowledge about urban food systems and experiences of household food insecurity in secondary African cities. With regard specifically to studies of food security in urban Malawi, the report builds on two previous AFSUN studies. The first was conducted as part of a regional 11-city baseline food security survey in Blantyre and provided a partial picture of the city through a geographical focus on a transitioning peri-urban area in South Lunzu Ward (Mvula and Chiweza, 2013). Relative to the low-income urban neighbourhoods in other Southern African cities, the Blantyre case study found high levels of food security and extremely high rates of households producing their own food (Frayne et al., 2010; Riley and Legwegoh, 2014). The second survey was conducted in 2015 in six informal neighbourhoods in Lilongwe and found extremely high rates of food insecurity (Chilanga et al., 2017). The difference with Blantyre was suggestive of a deteriorating situation due to the poor harvest in 2015 and the tumultuous political and economic changes in the country between 2008 and 2015, but was also reflective of differences between peri-urban areas and urban informal settlements within Malawi.

This report contributes to an understanding of poverty and sustainability in Mzuzu, Malawi, through the lens of household food security. Food connects economic, political, social, environmental, health, and cultural dimensions of the challenge of improving quality of life through development interventions (Frayne et al., 2018). The focus on food as an urban issue not only speaks to the development challenges presented by urbanization, but it also brings a fresh perspective to debates about food security in Malawi. Malawi is agriculturally rich and yet food security is a perennial problem to which solutions are typically framed in terms of rural development and agricultural innovation (Aberman et al., 2015).

The urban setting highlights the changing food system in Malawi where people in rural and urban areas are increasingly reliant on cash income to buy food. Urban food insecurity in Malawi is often juxtaposed with the periodic famines and absolute poverty found in rural areas and urban residents are assumed to have access to the abundance of food in markets (Riley, 2014; Legwegoh and Riley, 2014). Yet, the growth in Malawi's cities is almost entirely made up of people living in informal settlements with precarious income sources and a high level of vulnerability to food insecurity in the face of common risks such as morbidity and mortality due to HIV and AIDS, food price fluctuations, and inadequate income sources (Chilanga et al., 2017; Manda, 2013; UNHABITAT, 2011b).

The current survey in Mzuzu contributes further data to fill out this picture. It is the first city-wide household food security survey conducted in Malawi. It is also the first in a new AFSUN series on food systems in secondary cities, which places Mzuzu within the context of a regional trend of secondary urbanization that can help to broaden the scope for analytical insight and policy development. Indeed, the scope is made broader still by the context of the Sustainable Development Goals, which contain goals for food security and sustainable urbanization, and the New Urban Agenda unveiled at the 2016 Habitat III conference that provides a global vision for ecologically sustainable, prosperous, and socially-inclusive urbanization (Battersby. 2017; Crush and Riley, 2017). Actors at all scales emphasise the need for better data on secondary cities like Mzuzu, which are expanding rapidly and challenging conventional theories of urbanization through new types of built environments, new social organisations, and new urban food cultures (Roberts 2014; Satterthwaite 2006). The information in this report can be a key tool for policy makers, researchers, and civil society activists to steer the city's development in a positive direction aligned with the SDGs.

Section 2 provides an overview of Mzuzu. Section 3 outlines the methodology of the survey. Section 4 profiles the households included in the survey and characteristics of individual household members. Section 5 presents the survey findings regarding the economic conditions of the households. Section 6 includes the results of the household food security assessments and related information such as food responsibilities within households, the impact of food prices, and comparison with other AFSUN and Hungry Cities Partnership surveys. Section 7 profiles Mzuzu's food system from the point of view of households and highlights the multifaceted nature of a system that relies heavily on rural–urban linkages. It includes information about the use of various food sources, purchasing patterns for a select list of foods, household food production, food transfers, and the consumption of indigenous foods. Section 8 provides a brief summary of the report with key points for researchers and policy makers.

2. OVERVIEW OF MZUZU

Malawi is divided administratively into Northern, Central and Southern Regions and Mzuzu is the administrative centre for the Northern Region, which has a population of around 1.7 million (Manda, 2013) (Figure 1). It is the country's third largest city, although it is much smaller than Lilongwe, the capital, and Blantyre, the "commercial capital." The municipal boundaries encompass an area of about 144km^2 including forested and peri-urban areas. Mzuzu itself was established as a tung oil estate by the British government's Colonial Development Corporation in the 1950s in what was then an economically remote part of Nyasaland, known by colonial planners as the "Dead North" (McCracken, 2012). After the failure of the tung oil estate, the site was sold to the government and became an administrative hub of the Northern Region (Williams, 1969). It has grown rapidly in recent decades chiefly as a result of rural to urban migration within the Northern Region.

FIGURE 1: Map of Mzuzu

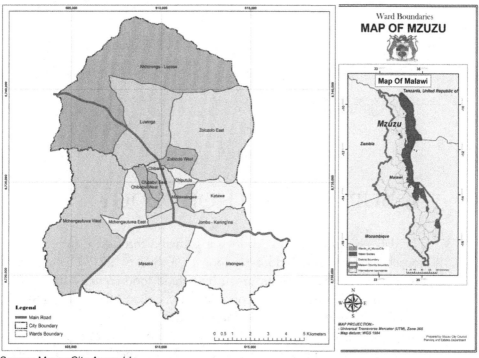

Source: Mzuzu City Assembly

Mzuzu was designated a city in 1985 as part of a national planning initiative to redirect urbanization away from the two main cities and to develop the economy of the Northern Region (Manda, 2013). Today, the north of the country enjoys some advantages relative to other areas, such as land abundance, high levels of education, and economic trade with East Africa via Tanzania. Mzuzu has been receiving increased investment and faces the benefits and challenges of rapid growth (Mambo and Malombe, 2014). Its population at the last census (2008) was 133,968, but with a rapid rate of growth, the population in 2020 is projected to double to 270,423 (UNHABITAT, 2011a) (Figure 2). With growth has come the expansion of informal settlements and the consequent problems of high rates of poverty and inequality and deteriorating environmental conditions (Kita, 2017; Gondwe and Ayenagbo, 2013).

FIGURE 2: The Growth of Mzuzu, 1966-2020

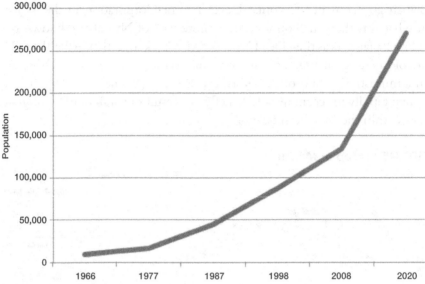

Source: Manda 2013; UNHABITAT 2011a

3. SURVEY METHODOLOGY

The data presented in this report was gathered through a survey of 910 households conducted door-to-door in February 2017. The survey instrument was based on an urban household food security survey first implemented by the African Food Security Urban Network (AFSUN) in 2008 (www.afsun.org/publications) and subsequently adapted by the Hungry Cities Partnership (HCP) (http://hungrycities.net/publications/). The survey instrument included sections about experiences indicative of food insecurity (including food security measurement tools developed by the Food and Nutrition Technical Assistance Project [FANTA]), access to basic goods and services, food sources, economic circumstances, and livelihood activities. The survey included questions about individual household members defined as people who eat from the same pot and sleep in the same dwelling and included children, babies and members of the household who are away for work (migrants) or for other reasons (with the stipulation that household members must reside in the dwelling for at least six months of the year on average).

The survey was translated into Chitumbuka, the predominant language of northern Malawi, and enumerators had access to the English and Chitumbuka versions of the survey on tablets programmed with Open Data Kit (ODK) software. The language environment in Mzuzu is complicated by the fact that Chitumbuka is a minority language in Malawi and as such it is not taught in school and is rarely written (Kamwendo, 2004). The situation is exacerbated by the linguistic diversity in Mzuzu. According to a 2006 survey by the University of Malawi, Mzuzu includes speakers of 20 indigenous languages (University of Malawi, 2006). There are significant communities of Chichewa, Chitonga, Chilambya, and Kiswahili speakers. Even in cases where the survey was conducted in languages other than Chitumbuka or English, the translator helped to ensure consistency by prompting discussions during the translation process and enumerator training about the underlying meanings of questions and their application in the local context.

The sampling method aimed to capture a city-wide representation of the population of Mzuzu (the area under the jurisdiction of the Mzuzu City Assembly). The sampling frame was based on the proportion of the population residing in each ward (determined by the population distribution by ward in the 2008 census and adjusted by an employee of the planning office based on local knowledge of which areas had grown in population relative to others). Enumerators from the University of Livingstonia interviewed an adult member of the household who was knowledgeable about income and expenditures and food purchasing practices in the household. Within each ward, multiple starting points were selected and small teams of enumerators were instructed to survey every third household along their sampling routes. The entire survey of Mzuzu was completed in 10 days of fieldwork. Figure 3 shows the spatial distribution of the sampled households.

The tablets allowed for recording the approximate GPS coordinates of each interview, which allowed for daily adjustments to the sampling strategy based on coverage observed on maps produced on a daily basis. The tablets also facilitated daily scrutiny of the data and follow-up conversations with enumerators and back-checking where problems appeared to emerge. These activities enhanced the coverage of the sample and the quality of the data set. Even with these advantages, the sampling strategy faced various logistical constraints including the lack of recent census information and the absence of house numbers or street names in informal settlements. The selection strategy on the ground naturally constrains the extent to which the data presented in this report are fully representative of the city of Mzuzu as a whole.

FIGURE 3: Spatial Distribution of Surveyed Households in the City of Mzuzu

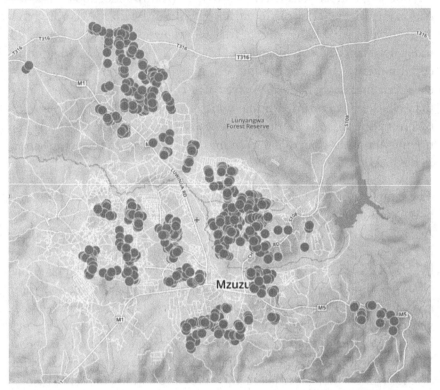

4. Household Characteristics

4.1. Household Size

The mean household size was 4.8, which is lower than both previous AFSUN surveys (5.3 in Lilongwe informal settlements in 2015 and 5.2 in Blantyre's transitional peri-urban community). This is partly explained by the inclusion of a greater range of households in this survey, including middle-class households that are likely to be smaller. About one in six households had one or two members while more than half of the households (56%) had three, four or five members (Figure 4). The largest household had 24 members, and fewer than 4% had 10 or more members.

FIGURE 4: Household Size

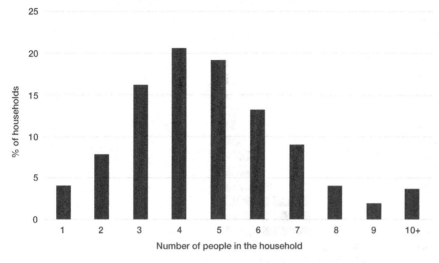

4.2. Age of Household Members

The population pyramid for Mzuzu shows the age group distribution for males and females (Figure 5). There are more male than female children under age five and there is virtually the same percentage of males and females from ages 5 to 19. While more women are in their 20s, men make up a greater share of all age groups from 35 to 69. More women than men are aged 70 and above. The male bias of those between the ages of 35 and 69 could be a legacy of the past when cities were associated with men seeking work, while women and children stayed in the rural areas (McCracken, 2012; Vaughan, 1987). The generational shift is part of a change toward gender balance in urban Malawi that was already evident in the 2008 census when the gender ratio in Mzuzu shifted from 106.4 in 1998 to 100.6 in 2008 (Manda, 2013: 6). The idea that urbanization was a temporary male migration has historically been used to justify a lack of investment in social infrastructure in Southern African cities (Vaughan, 1987). Finding gender parity for younger age groups suggests that more people are born in the city and that families are based there, and reinforces the need for investment in urban social services.

FIGURE 5: Population Pyramid of Household Members

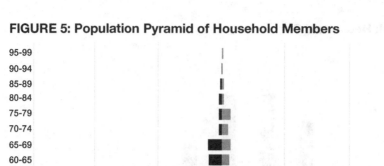

The ages of household heads provide further insight into the population and how households are organized in Mzuzu. More than half (57%) of the household heads were in the age range of 26 to 40 and nearly a quarter (23%) were slightly older (aged 41 to 55) (Figure 6). Twelve percent were over 55 and 9% were under 26.

FIGURE 6: Age of Household Heads

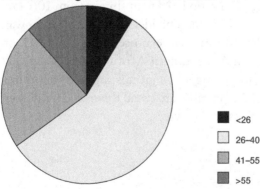

4.3. Migrant Households

Mzuzu's population growth is largely due to migration into the city from other parts of Malawi. Figure 7 provides a snapshot of one type of "migrant household" defined as households with a head born somewhere other than in Mzuzu. The largest share (41%) of household heads were born in "a rural area in Malawi." Only 29% of heads were born in Mzuzu and 27% were born in another urban area in Malawi. The remaining 2% were born outside Malawi.

FIGURE 7: Birthplace of Household Heads

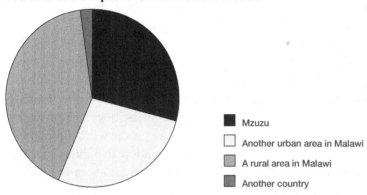

The link between birthplace of the head and the migrant status of the household can be mitigated by factors such as the length of time the household has been in Mzuzu and the birthplace of other household members. Table 1 provides further insight by providing the mean age of household heads according to birthplace. The youngest group on average were those born in another urban area in Malawi (36.4), followed by those born in Mzuzu (38.5), rural areas in Malawi (40.9) and another country (46.2) (Table 1). This could point to a growing trend of inter-urban migration among households headed by younger people. Taking into account all individuals for whom data was recorded, the average age for people born in Mzuzu was very young (16.2). The next youngest group on average were those born in another urban area in Malawi (27.1), a rural area in Malawi (30.5), and another country (41.2). The observation that people born in Mzuzu are by far the youngest group highlights the fact that the high rate of growth is not only due to migration but also natural growth of the urban population.

TABLE 1: Age and Place of Birth		
Place of birth	Mean age of household heads	Mean age of all individuals
Mzuzu	38.5	16.2
Another urban area in Malawi	36.4	27.1
A rural area in Malawi	40.9	30.5
Another country	44.6	41.2

4.4. Education Levels

The education levels of household members are presented in Figure 8, disaggregated by the relationship to the household head, age group, and gender. A higher proportion of female household heads than male heads reported not having any formal education (14% and 4% respectively). Among household heads, only about half of women had some secondary or post-secondary education compared to 72% of men. Among women, female heads have a greater likelihood of having no formal education than female spouses (5%). A possible explanation is that the former includes older widows who were raised at a time before gender parity in education was common, even though women in northern Malawi have tradition-ally had more access to formal education than women in other regions (Kadzamira and Rose, 2001). In the youth categories, boys and girls have relatively close parity in education. In fact, the group with the highest likelihood of some post-secondary education is adult daughters (a third have some post-secondary education compared to about a quarter of adult sons).

FIGURE 8: Education Levels of Household Members by Gender and Relationship to the Household Head

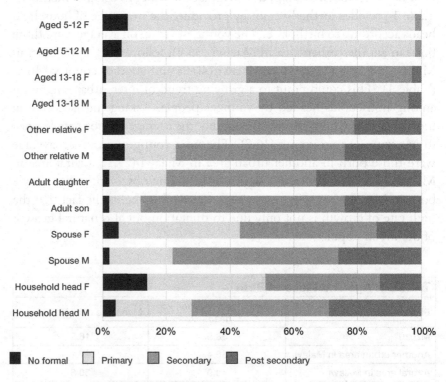

4.5. Household Composition

The survey used the AFSUN household types to assign each household to one of five categories defined by the composition of members and their relationships to one another (Frayne et al., 2010). This typology aims to move beyond the male-headed/female-headed binary often used in household food security research and capture more of the dynamics that shape households. Female-centred and male-centred households include a head without a spouse or partner and any other combination of children, relatives, and other members. They are distinguished from each other by the gender of the head. Nuclear and extended households include a head with a spouse or partner. The distinguishing feature between these two types is that the nuclear household only includes children as additional members, whereas extended households include others, e.g. parents or siblings of the head of the household, other relatives, or non-relatives. The fifth type is a single person living alone. Nuclear households were the most common type in Mzuzu (49%), with extended households the second most common (26%). There were more female-centred (16%) than male-centred (6%) households and very few single-person households (2%) (Figure 9).

FIGURE 9: Household Type

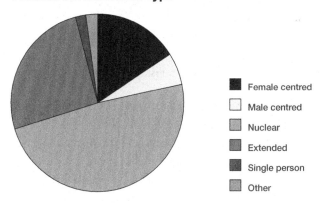

5. POVERTY AND LIVELIHOODS

Malawi is one of the poorest countries in the world in terms of GDP per capita at USD300.30 in 2016 (World Bank, 2018). It is difficult to quantify the urban poverty rate by conventional economic metrics because of the high cost of living in cities relative to the rural areas and the inconsistency of many household incomes earned through the informal economy (Manda, 2013). There are also consistent challenges in collecting income data (i.e. lack of knowledge among respondents, irregularity of incomes, lack of accounting from multiple income sources, unwillingness to share income data, and a general tendency to overestimate expenses and underestimate income). As a result, the data in this section is based on a subsample of the survey population because only 37% of respondents shared income data. With this limitation in mind, the data provides a window, albeit partially obscured, into the economic reality of households in Mzuzu.

5.1. Household Income and Expenditure

Informal wage work (earning money by working for an entity not recognized by the government) was the main source of income of households in Mzuzu (reported by 42%) (Figure 10). The second most widely reported income source was formal wage work (earning a regular salary from an entity recognized by the government) (23%). Figure 10 includes "net income" (NI) from various types of business activities. Thirteen percent reported income from a formal business. Income from informal business was divided into several sub-categories. The most prevalent type of informal business income was from the sale of goods (10% of households), followed by the production and sale of fresh produce (6%) and the sale of produce not produced by the household (4%). Both "other kinds" of informal business and renting property were reported by 2% of households. The sum of these percentages does not account for households with multiple types of informal businesses; however, a separate calculation found that 22% households had an income from at least one informal business (income sources indicated with an asterisk in Figure 10).

The average income received in the previous month was 93,251 Malawian kwacha (USD131)[1]. The median income of MWK30,000 (USD42) was less than a third of the mean figure. The gap between mean and median suggests that the typical income level is far below the mean. Combined with a standard deviation of 262,286, there is clearly an extremely wide variation in incomes. The variability of incomes is evident in the distribution of income quintiles that indicate that one-fifth of households had incomes of MWK8,000 (USD11.20) per month or less while the cut-off for the highest quintile was 12.5 times higher at MWK100,000 (USD140) (Table 2).

FIGURE 10: Household Income Sources in the Previous Month

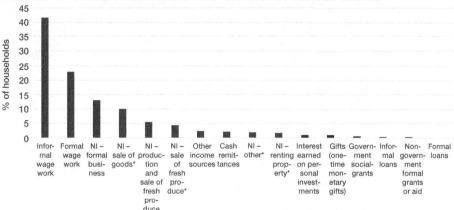

Note: Multiple-response question
* = types of informal business

TABLE 2: Household Incomes		
Income quintiles	MWK	USD
1	<=8000	<=11.20
2	8,001-25,000	11.21-35.00
3	25,001-50,000	35.01-70.00
4	50,001-100,000	70.01-140.00
5	>100,000	>140.00
Mean income	93,251	131
Median income	30,000	42

The amount of income earned from each source provides an additional vantage point for understanding income levels in Mzuzu (Table 3). The mean income from formal wage work is MWK121,749 (USD170), but with a standard deviation of 256,201 it is apparent that the mean is inflated by a small number of very high earners. The same is true for other apparently lucrative income sources such as renting property and formal business. In the case of formal wage work, for example, about half (49%) of incomes were MWK50,000 (USD70) or less.

Food and groceries represented the most commonly identified household expenditure in the previous month (94% of households) (Figure 11). The second most common expenditure was fuel (59%) and the third was education (53%). Slightly more than half of the households said that they spent money on housing.

TABLE 3: Average Monthly Income by Income Source				
Income source	No. of households reporting income	Mean (MWK)	Mean (USD)	Standard deviation (MWK)
Informal work	117	41,842	59	64,873
Formal wage work	87	121,749	170	256,201
Net income from formal business	57	144,316	202	309,725
Net income from informal business (sale of goods)	33	29,967	42	43,799
Net income from informal business (production and sale of fresh produce by this household)	18	44,861	63	68,989
Cash remittances (regular financial support from friends or family)	13	51,615	72	55,167
Net income from informal business (sale of fresh produce not produced by this household)	12	26,683	37	32,023
Net income from informal business (renting property)	12	215,500	302	625,603

FIGURE 11: Types of Monthly Expenditure

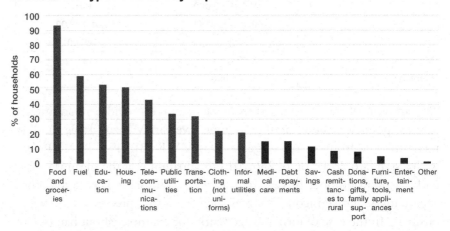

Table 4 provides additional information on household expenditures, including how much was spent on each category, ordered from most to least expensive item on average. As with income questions, many households did not report expenses. The most notable absence was on food and groceries, for which 94% said they incurred the expense but only 43% of these households also provided information about their monthly food and groceries expenditures. There are several plausible explanations, including a lack of record keeping, many people in the household buying groceries, and monthly fluctuations in the cost of food. Bearing in mind the limitations due to low response rates, Table 4 gives a sense of how expensive various items can be in Mzuzu relative to incomes. The cost of education was most expensive, but a high standard deviation suggests that the mean is high because some households incur abnormally high expenses for education, perhaps with members attending university or private school.

TABLE 4: Monthly Household Expenditures				
Household expenditure	No. of households reporting expense	Mean expense (MWK)	Mean expense (USD)	Standard deviation (MWK)
Education (tuition, books, uniforms, excludes insurance)	403	49,459	69	100,787
Savings	66	42,112	59	54,933
Food and groceries	369	25,984	37	37,414
Debt repayments	112	23,356	33	55,426
Cash remittances to rural areas	56	22,593	32	24,975
Housing (rent, mortgage payments, maintenance, renovation)	418	17,350	24	27,657
Medical care (doctor's visits, medications, supports, excludes insurance)	80	13,824	19	46,887
Clothing (excluding uniforms)	104	10,362	15	13,277
Donations, gifts, family support (only to other households)	51	8,785	12	13,512
Transportation (purchase of cars, motorbikes, bicycles; maintenance, fuel; public transit; not insurance)	164	8,591	12	13,513
Publicly provided utilities (water, electricity, sanitation, plus all taxes)	264	7,555	11	7,694
Informally purchased utilities (water, electricity, sanitation)	154	7,503	11	9,640
Fuel (firewood, charcoal, paraffin, kerosene, propane)	417	5,618	8	10,244
Telecommunications (cellphone, telephone, internet)	214	4,699	7	14,323

The low response rate for income and expenditure questions makes it difficult to draw conclusions about the economic dimensions of food at the household scale. Food and groceries was the third most expensive budget item on average at MWK25,984 (USD37) (Table 4). Figure 12 provides some insight into the cost of food and groceries based on the 213 households (23% of all households) for which both income data and food expenditure data were available. Calculations were made using mean and median household incomes and amounts spent on food and groceries for the cost of food as a percentage of income for each wealth category. A linear correlation appears whereby low-income households spent a far higher percentage of their income on food and groceries than high-income households.

FIGURE 12: Food and Groceries Expense by Income Quintile

When the mean values are used, the percentage among first and second quintile households exceeds 100%. This trend is not new within poverty studies where low-income households often exceed their incomes to meet their basic needs. For example, a 1991 study in Blantyre and Lilongwe found that low-income households spent more on food than they reported receiving in income (Chilowa, 1991: 7):

> Looking at income groups individually the figures show that over eighty per cent of those who receive an income of less than [MW] K40.00 stated that they spent more than they earned on food alone, with the average monthly food expenditure in this group being [MW] K43.00. Incongruous as this finding may appear, it should not be surprising. The households which fall into this category survive on a hand to mouth basis, they are involved in various credit arrangements, small businesses and sometimes *katangale*. They also rely more on non-cash income.

In terms of the ratio between mean values, the percentage spent on food and groceries by households in the first quintile is 10 times the percentage spent by households in the fifth quintile (162% and 16% respectively). In the ratio based on median values, the difference is smaller, but is still five times higher for the first quintile (100% and 20% respectively). In both mean and median measurements, the largest quintile-to-quintile gap is between the first and second, which reflects the exceptionally difficult circumstances of Mzuzu's ultra-poor.

5.2. Work Status

Among those household members over the age of 18, the most common work status was self-employment (26%) (Figure 13). Only 15% of adult household members were working full-time, which reflects the high rates of unemployment and the economic precarity of most households. Figure 14 provides a point of comparison based on government statistics collected in 2013 for people aged 15-64 in all of urban Malawi. By combining certain categories in both figures, the distribution of work status is remarkably similar: students, pensioners, and medically unfit (18%) relative to non-participants (15%); family worker, unemployed/looking for work, and unemployed/not looking for work (30%) relative to unemployed (33%); self-employed (26%) relative to own-account worker, family worker, and employer (26%); and working full-time and working part-time, casual, or seasonal (25%) relative to paid employee (27%).

FIGURE 13: Work Status Among Household Members Over 18

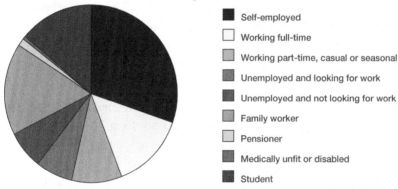

FIGURE 14: Employment of People Aged 15-64 in Urban Malawi, 2013

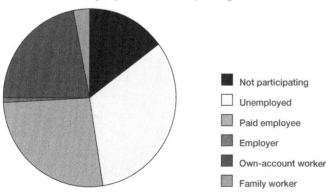

Source: Government of Malawi 2016.

5.3. Housing Types

Noting that the income poverty line in Malawi is one-quarter of the international benchmark of USD1 per day, Manda (2013: 33) argued that "the claim that only 7.5% (2005) and 4.3% (2011) of the urban population can be ultra-poor is a gross underestimation of the situation." He drew attention instead to the UNHABITAT figures of 60%-70% of urban Malawians living in slum conditions as a better approximation of the extent of poverty in urban Malawi. In keeping with Manda's argument that income data only tells part of the story of urban poverty, this section supplements the income data with information about housing in Mzuzu. In the course of translating the survey instrument into Chitumbuka, a series of definitions of different housing types were developed to reflect different standards of living within the city:

- "House" refers to a typical house in the local context, meaning that the kitchen and bathroom are outside (*Nyumba yamalata kwene ya khichini, bafa na chimbuzi chakuwalo*);

- "Townhouse" refers to a higher quality house where the kitchen and bathroom are inside (*Nyumba yachitauni ya bafa, khicheni na toilet yamukati mwa nyumba*);

- "Traditional dwelling/homestead" is built with traditional/locally made bricks and has a grass thatched roof (*Nyumba yautheka*);

- "Shack in informal settlement" refers to housing structures that are usually less permanent than a "traditional dwelling/homestead" and built with a variety of provisional materials including timber, plastic bags, and plastic sheets (*Chisakasa*);

- "Backyard shack attached to house" coincides with what is locally known as "boy's quarters";

- "Other" included a range of options, such as apartments, hotels, and mobile homes.

The most common type of dwelling was a house (50%), followed by townhouse (25%) (Figure 15). Eighteen percent were living in traditional dwellings/homesteads and 3% each were living in backyard shacks and in shacks in squatter camps. Only 2% lived in another type of housing. These findings indicate that the vast majority of households in Mzuzu do not have the convenience of indoor running water. They also reflect that, even in the city, many people occupy houses made from traditional materials that are typically associated with rural dwellings.

FIGURE 15: Housing Types

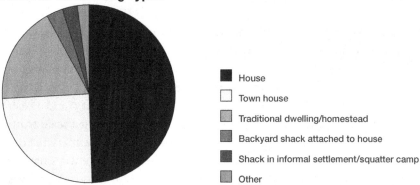

The link between income poverty and housing type is evident in the analysis presented in Figure 16. Households in the fourth and fifth quintiles are much more likely to occupy townhouses and therefore have the most convenient access to indoor amenities. On the other hand, households in the second and third quintiles are the most likely to live in traditional dwellings/homesteads, suggesting that these houses are not only for the poorest households. Rather, they are occupied by many middle and lower-middle income households.

FIGURE 16: Housing Types by Income Quintile

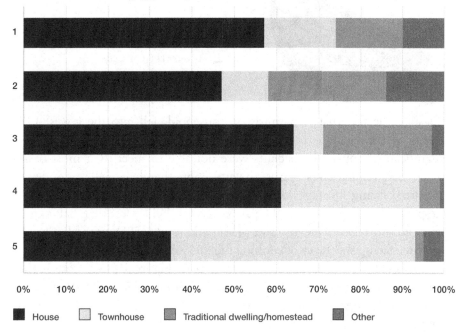

5.4. Lived Poverty Index

The Lived Poverty Index (LPI) measures how frequently (never, just once or twice, several times, many times, or always) people report going without a basket of basic necessities in the previous 12 months (Afrobarometer 2004, Rose 1998). The items measured include food, clean water, medicine and medical treatment, fuel to cook food, electricity, and a cash income. An LPI score is calculated for each household along a scale from zero to four, with zero being the least poor (never having experienced a lack of access to all basic necessities) and four the poorest (always having experienced a lack of access). The mean score for Mzuzu households was 0.8, the minimum was zero, and the maximum 3.5. By way of comparison, the mean score in South Lunzu, Blantyre, in 2008 was 0.9 (Frayne et al., 2010). Figure 17 shows the breakdown of scores into four LPI categories: low (67%), moderate (26%), high (6%), and extremely high (0.4%).

FIGURE 17: LPI Categories

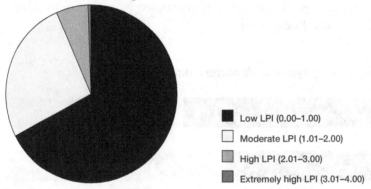

Low LPI (0.00–1.00)

Moderate LPI (1.01–2.00)

High LPI (2.01–3.00)

Extremely high LPI (3.01–4.00)

Despite the fact that two-thirds of households fell into the lowest LPI category, the responses to the individual lived poverty questions show that significant numbers of residents were not able to meet their most basic needs on a regular basis. Across the city, more than half of all respondents reported facing shortages of electricity and cash income (77% and 53% respectively at least once in the past year) and slightly less than half experienced shortages of clean water (42%) and food (45%), with about one in three facing shortages of cooking fuel (33%) and medicine and medical services (31%) at least once in the past year (Figure 18). Of note is the intensity of deprivation: a high proportion of households faced repeated shortages (going without "many times" or "always" in the past year) with respect to electricity (51%), cash income (22%), food (18%), and water (16%). Only 24% had consistent electricity access. While electricity was the most common inaccessible need, the high rates of shortage of cash income is arguably more concerning because of the need for cash to support all aspects of urban life.

FIGURE 18: Lived Poverty Experience

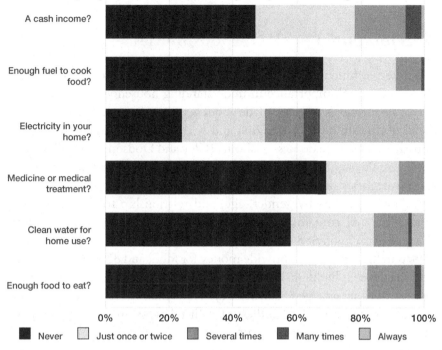

Over the past year, how often, if ever, have you or your household gone without:

A cash income?

Enough fuel to cook food?

Electricity in your home?

Medicine or medical treatment?

Clean water for home use?

Enough food to eat?

0%   20%   40%   60%   80%   100%

■ Never   ☐ Just once or twice   ■ Several times   ■ Many times   ☐ Always

A focus on aggregate LPI scores often hides considerable inter-household differences. Table 5 provides a breakdown of mean LPI based on the gender and age of the household head. The mean LPI for households headed by men and women is exactly the same (0.81). However, female-headed households have a greater deviation from the mean (0.79) compared to male-headed households (0.70), indicating that inequalities in access to basic necessities are more pronounced among households headed by women. LPI is also influenced by the age of the household head. Households headed by young people (under 30 years) experienced the highest average LPI (0.87). Households with middle-aged (30-55 years) and elderly (>55 years) heads have lower average LPIs (0.78 and 0.79 respectively), showing that they are less exposed to deprivation of basic needs.

TABLE 5: LPI Scores by Characteristics of Household Heads

Characteristic of household head		Mean LPI	Median LPI	Standard deviation
Gender	Female	.81	.67	.79
	Male	.81	.67	.70
Age	Young (<30)	.87	.83	.77
	Middle (30-55)	.78	.67	.71
	Older (>55)	.79	.67	.77
All		.83	.67	.72

6. HOUSEHOLD FOOD INSECURITY

6.1. Household Food Responsibilities

The internal functioning of the household to obtain, prepare and serve food is of central importance in understanding household food security. While assumptions are often made about gendered household roles, urban social norms are rapidly changing and with this are changes in the way households organize domestic labour (Riley and Dodson, 2016). To contextualize the significance of five food-related activities in relation to the social categories of different household members, Table 6 disaggregates household members by gender, age, and relationship to the household head. Each cell contains the percentage of people in the row category engaged in each activity. For example, among female heads of households, 70% purchase food, 65% provide money for food, and 82% prepare food. The shaded cells highlight instances where the majority of individuals in a row category are engaged in an activity. Thus, the majority of women and girls over the age of 12, regardless of their relationship to the household head, are engaged in preparing food.

	Relationship to household head	Purchas-ing food	Providing money for food	Prepar-ing food	Deciding who will get food	Growing food	Does none of these
TABLE 6: Engagement in Food-Related Activities by Gender, Age and Relationship to Household Head							
Female	Head	70	65	82	29	20	3
	Spouse/partner	72	38	98	26	25	1
	Daughter (>18)	37	19	82	9	19	11
	Other relative (>18)	15	24	78	27	8	16
	Non-relative (>18)	30	14	95	0	23	5
	Aged 13-18	21	0.6	76	13	8	22
	Aged 5-12	8	0.4	27	2	2	69
Male	Head	77	94	18	5	18	3
	Spouse/partner	87	92	15	6	17	4
	Son (>18)	39	22	34	8	17	33
	Other relative (>18)	30	39	32	5	7	27
	Non-relative (>18)	36	27	55	0	18	18
	Aged 13-18	18	2	36	8	13	53
	Aged 5-12	7	0	8	1	1	86

The only row category of men with a majority engaged in preparing food are adult non-relatives. Men who are heads of their households or spouses of the head of the household are likely to be purchasing food and providing money to buy food. One of the most striking contrasts is between adolescent girls and boys. A majority of adolescent boys (53%) are not engaged in any food-related activities, compared with only 22% of girls. Even among children aged 5-12, there are more boys (86%) than girls (69%) not engaged in food-related activities. The implication is that gender roles continue to be highly pronounced, perhaps reducing the time that girls have to allocate to their studies and to recreational pursuits.

6.2. Household Food Insecurity

The Household Food Insecurity Access Scale (HFIAS) measures the degree of food insecurity during the four weeks prior to the survey using nine frequency-of-occurrence questions (Coates et al., 2007). The minimum possible score is 0, meaning that the household never experienced any of the events, and the maximum is 27, meaning that all events were experienced often. The higher the score, the more food insecurity the household experienced. The mean score in Mzuzu was 6.7 and the median was 5 (see section 6.8 for comparative data with other cities). The gap between the mean and the median reflects the minority of households with extremely high scores that raised the average (19% had scores above 12) (Figure 19). At the same time, 40% of households had very low scores of three or below and therefore rarely experienced food insecurity. The wide range in scores illustrated in Figure 19 is part of an overall picture of inequality in a secondary city where some households frequently experience food insecurity while others rarely have difficulty in accessing food.

FIGURE 19: Distribution of HFIAS Scores

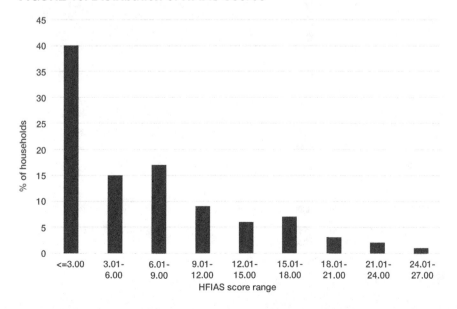

The responses to each of the nine HFIAS questions help to convey the types of events that households in Mzuzu experienced. Most respondents said that their households experienced the following in the four weeks prior to the survey: worrying that the household would not have enough food (62%); someone in the household being unable to eat the kinds of foods they preferred because of a lack of resources (60%); eating a limited variety of foods because of a lack of resources (60%), and eating some foods that they really did not want to eat because of a lack of resources to obtain other kinds of food (60%) (Figure 20). Slightly fewer than half of the households experienced the following: eating a smaller meal than they felt they needed (49%) and eating fewer meals in a day because there was not enough food (46%).

The remaining three events, which are more severe examples of food insecurity, were experienced by a minority of households but still widespread among a sizeable segment of the population: 41% had no food of any kind to eat in the household because of a lack of money to buy food; 32% had a household member go to sleep at night hungry because there was not enough food; and 26% had a member go a whole day and night without eating anything because there was not enough food. Only 2% of households "often" had a member go a whole day and night without eating. While this appears to be a small percentage, if extrapolated to the whole population of the city it could mean that several thousand people in Mzuzu are often going a whole day and night without eating anything.

FIGURE 20: Frequency of Experience of Food Insecurity

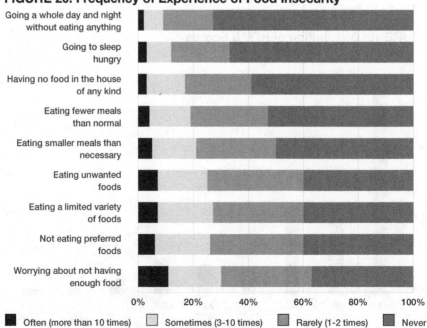

The Household Food Insecurity Access Prevalence (HFIAP) indicator provides a tool that helps account for the different levels of severity of the experiences captured in the HFIAS score. The HFIAP groups households into four levels of household food insecurity: food secure, mildly food insecure, moderately food insecure, and severely food insecure (Coates et al., 2007). The largest share of Mzuzu households are in the severely food insecure category (45%) (Figure 21). Again reflecting the high degree of inequality in the city, the second largest share was food secure (28%). The remaining households were mildly food insecure (12%) or moderately food insecure (15%).

FIGURE 21: Household Food Insecurity Access Prevalence

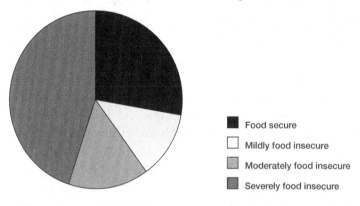

6.3. Household Dietary Diversity

The Household Dietary Diversity Score (HDDS) captures up to 12 food groups consumed by household members in the previous 24 hours (Swindale and Bilinsky, 2006). An increase in the average number of different food groups consumed provides a quantifiable measure of greater household dietary diversity and is suggestive of better nutrition. The mean score in Mzuzu was 6.2 (standard deviation of 2.44) and the median was 6. The minimum was zero (meaning that a household had not consumed any food from the 12 food groups in the previous 24 hours) and the maximum was 12. Figure 23 illustrates the distribution of HDDS. About one-third of households had an HDDS of 6 or 7, slightly less than a third (30%) had favourable scores higher than 7, and more than a third (38%) had scores lower than 6.

FIGURE 22: Household Dietary Diversity Score Distribution

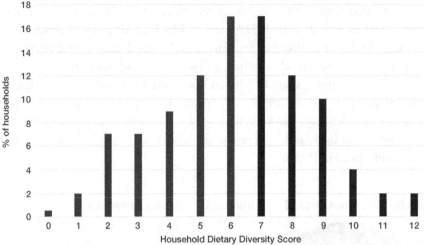

The food groups are designed to capture a variety of nutritional contributions to the household diet, so a higher HDDS does not necessarily mean better nutrition if the additional foods being consumed are less nutritious or related to health problems, as in the case of sugar and its link to obesity and diabetes (Legwegoh and Riley, 2014). Almost all households consumed foods made from grains (94%) and vegetables (89%) (Figure 23). The next three most commonly consumed food groups were "foods made from oil, fat, or butter," sugar or honey, and "other foods such as condiments, coffee or tea." These categories primarily contribute energy to the diet and offer relatively little protein and micronutrients. More than half of the households consumed fruit (54%). Fish is the main source of protein, consumed by 45% of households. An equal number of households consumed meat and dairy products (29%) and root vegetables and beans and nuts (24%). The least widely consumed food group was eggs (21%).

6.4. Household Monthly Food Provisioning

The Months of Adequate Household Food Provisioning (MAHFP) assessment tool captures the household's access to food on a monthly basis (Bilinsky and Swindale, 2007). The implementation of the MAHFP in Mzuzu focused on months in the previous year when it was difficult to access food when compared to the benchmark of the household's normal food access. The final MAHFP score is calculated as 12 minus the number of months during which the household experienced a lack of adequate food provisioning. The mean MAHFP score for Mzuzu was 11.0 and the median 12 (standard deviation 1.44). The minimum was 0 and the maximum 12. Only two households had a score of 0 and fewer than 3% had scores below 8. About half (51%) scored 12 (Figure 24).

FIGURE 23: Food Groups Consumed in the Previous 24 Hours

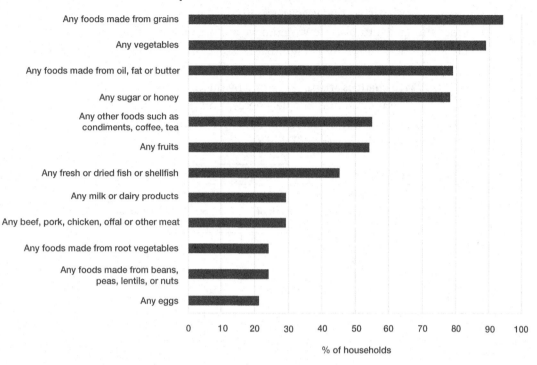

FIGURE 24: MAHFP Scores

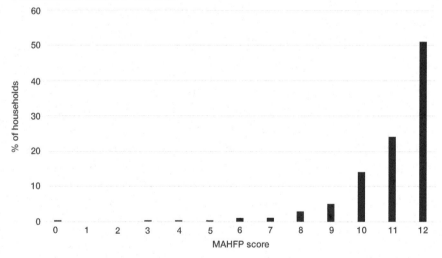

Previous research found different seasonal patterns of food inaccessibility in the MAHFP. For example, in a comparison of two surveys conducted in informal urban settlements in Harare, Zimbabwe, in 2008 and 2012, researchers observed a changing trend that appeared to correspond with a shift from a lack of access during the agricultural lean season before the harvest to the financial lean season at the beginning of the calendar year after holiday expenses and debt repayment (Tawodzera et al., 2016). The

Mzuzu survey aimed to capture more detail about the reasons for seasonal food insecurity in secondary cities, with the expectation that in secondary cities the agricultural cycle would have a more prominent impact than in primary cities. Table 7 illustrates that lack of cash and food prices were the first and second most important reasons for not accessing food in every month. Price changes are partly caused by fluctuations in supply related to the agricultural cycle, but people's perception of why they cannot access food is more strongly associated with the difficulty of cash transactions than with agriculture per se (Table 8).

Month	% of households not accessing adequate food	% agreeing with reason for not accessing food			
		Lack of cash	Food price	Agricultural cycle	Other reason
January	58	94	36	9	4
February	48	93	36	11	5
March	15	96	33	15	3
April	5	100	38	8	4
May	2	100	44	11	0
June	3	82	18	9	9
July	3	91	18	9	9
August	6	88	28	8	16
September	4	90	26	5	11
October	10	85	39	9	9
November	15	90	34	7	4
December	23	94	26	7	3

TABLE 7: Frequency and Reasons for Food Inaccessibility by Month

For each reason given for each month, the respondent was asked what foods were inaccessible from a list of food types based on the HDDS list. Table 8 presents the results for the month of January, which was selected because it was the month with the highest percentage of households experiencing food inadequacy (58%). There were some strong consistencies in the most and least commonly cited foods that were inaccessible: "food made from grains," meat, and dairy products were the top three foods for all three reasons (lack of cash, food price, and the agricultural cycle). Vegetables were the least likely to be inaccessible for all three reasons. "Sugar or honey," eggs, and "fish or shellfish" were much less likely to be cited as inaccessible because of the agricultural cycle than for other reasons, which reflects that these are items that are normally purchased and possibly more price sensitive.

TABLE 8: Foods that were Inaccessible in January Ranked by Reason for Inadequate Food Access

Rank	Reasons for inaccessibility		
	Lack of cash	Food price	Agricultural cycle
1	Food made from grains (77%)	Food made from grains (83%)	Food made from grains (68%)
2	Meat (77%)	Meat (81%)	Meat (55%)
3	Dairy products (53%)	Dairy products (64%)	Dairy products (50%)
4	Sugar or honey (42%)	Root vegetables and tubers (56%)	Root vegetables and tubers (50%)
5	Root vegetables and tubers (41%)	Fish or shellfish (51%)	Food made from beans, nuts, etc (23%)
6	Food made from oil (39%)	Eggs (48%)	Food made from oil (23%)
7	Fish or shellfish (39%)	Sugar or honey (45%)	Fish or shellfish (18%)
8	Eggs (38%)	Food made from oil (45%)	Eggs (18%)
9	Food made from beans, nuts, etc (27%)	Food made from beans, nuts, etc (32%)	Fruit (14%)
10	Condiments, coffee, tea, etc (21%)	Condiments, coffee, tea, etc (28%)	Sugar or honey (14%)
11	Fruit (17%)	Fruit (26%)	Condiments, coffee, tea, etc (13%)
12	Vegetables (6%)	Vegetables (12%)	Vegetables (9%)

6.5. Food Prices

More than half of the surveyed households (57%) in Mzuzu had gone without certain types of food due to food prices in the six months prior to the survey (Figure 25). Twenty-nine percent went without food due to food prices on a monthly basis, 19% on a weekly basis, 8% more than once a week but less than daily, and 1% on a daily basis.

Meat was the most cited food that people went without because it was unaffordable (Figure 26). The second most frequently unaffordable food was food made from grains. All other food groups were cited by a minority of households affected by food price. As in Table 8, vegetables were the least likely food to be inaccessible due to price (only 3% of households).

FIGURE 25: Frequency of Going Without Foods Because of the Price

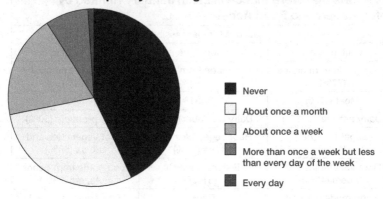

- ■ Never
- □ About once a month
- ▨ About once a week
- ▨ More than once a week but less than every day of the week
- ■ Every day

FIGURE 26: Food Categories Deemed Unaffordable

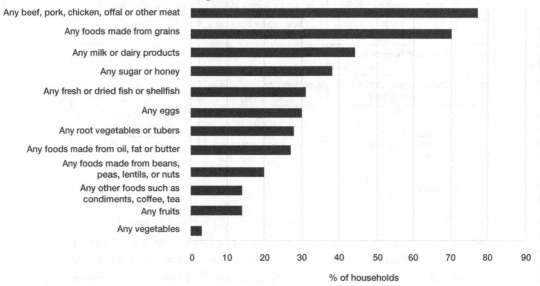

6.6. Food Security and Household Characteristics

The relationship between household food security scores and household type is illustrated in Table 9. Female-centred households had the lowest dietary diversity (as measured by the HDDS), lowest rates of month-to-month stability (lowest MAHFP) and highest level of food insecurity (highest mean HFIAS score). The mean HFIAS score among female-centred households (9.0) was almost double that of male-centred households (4.7). Single-person households had the second lowest mean HFIAS score (5.1), and nuclear (6.3) and extended (6.9) households were between the extremes of the male and female-centred households. The high standard deviation in the HFIAS scores suggests a wide variation in all categories. Of note is the median HFIAS score of 0 among male-centred households, of which 55% had scores of 0.0, despite a median

HDDS score in line with other household types. This combination of findings suggests that male-centred households tend to have little nutritional advantage despite having better access to food.

TABLE 9: Food Security Scores by Household Type

Household structure		HDDS	HFIAS	MAHFP
Female centred	Mean	5.7	9.0	10.8
	Median	6.0	9.0	11.0
	Standard deviation	2.45	7.47	1.40
Male centred	Mean	6.7	4.7	11.5
	Median	6.0	0.0	12.0
	Standard deviation	2.39	6.89	0.99
Nuclear	Mean	6.2	6.3	11.1
	Median	6.0	5.0	12.0
	Standard deviation	2.45	6.06	1.39
Extended	Mean	6.3	6.9	11.0
	Median	6.0	6.0	12.0
	Standard deviation	2.30	6.51	1.53
Single person	Mean	6.5	5.1	11.3
	Median	6.0	4.0	12.0
	Standard deviation	2.76	6.52	1.26

Gender is linked to food security in several ways, for example through the lower earning power of women in the labour market, the caregiver role that often leads to women being heads of households with many dependants, and, in terms of men's disadvantages, their inferior knowledge of food and cooking skills (Dodson et al., 2012). Table 10 presents analysis of the gender and the age of the household head. The mean HFIAS score among households headed by women (7.6) was higher than for households headed by men (6.1). The gap in HDDS and MAHFP was far smaller, with equivalent median scores in both columns. Notably, households with a female head had a lower mean HFIAS score than female-centred households, suggesting that female heads with spouses, which make up 36% of female heads, have an advantage over single women heading households (by definition, heads of female-centred households do not have spouses).

In terms of the age of the household head, households with older heads (over 55 years old) had the highest mean HFIAS score (7.9), followed by middle-aged (6.4) and young heads (6.0) (Table 10). In contrast to the HFIAS score gap, the median HDDS was again the same (at 6), suggesting that food insecure households headed by older people are able to ensure a level of dietary diversity on a par with more food secure households headed by younger people. This could also be suggestive of a narrow diet pursued by younger household heads, which would be consistent with urbanization, convenience, and an emphasis on processed foods. These findings resonate with analysis of AFSUN data and merit further investigation (Riley and Legwegoh, 2018).

TABLE 10: Food Security Scores by Gender and Age of Household Head				
Household head characteristics		HDDS	HFIAS	MAHFP
Woman	Mean	5.9	7.6	11.0
	Median	6.0	8.0	12.0
	Standard deviation	2.73	7.05	1.40
Man	Mean	6.3	6.1	11.0
	Median	6.0	5.0	12.0
	Standard deviation	2.45	6.24	1.42
Young (<30)	Mean	6.2	6.0	11.3
	Median	6.0	4.0	12.0
	Standard deviation	2.69	6.81	1.14
Middle (30-55)	Mean	6.3	6.4	10.9
	Median	6.0	5.0	11.0
	Standard deviation	2.45	6.34	1.56
Older (>55)	Mean	5.9	7.9	10.8
	Median	6.0	7.0	11.0
	Standard deviation	2.42	6.83	1.54

6.7. Food Security and Income Sources

It is generally assumed that income and food security are positively correlated, given the importance of money for accessing food in urban settings. Table 11 reveals that in Mzuzu, the relationship is not straightforward. On the HFIAS, MAHFP, and LPI scores, the lowest income quintile had better mean scores than the second lowest income quintile. On MAHFP, the lowest income quintile had a slightly better score than even the third quintile. It is only in these lower income ranges that the positive correlation between income and food security is interrupted; the second, third, fourth and fifth quintiles consistently decrease in mean HFIAS score (Table 11). It is plausible in Mzuzu that some households with low incomes are successful subsistence farmers and therefore generally food secure without the need for much money to buy food. Other mitigating factors could be households that do not have to pay for housing, households receiving food remittances, and other non-monetary ways of obtaining food.

TABLE 11: Food Security Scores by Income Quintile

Income quintile	Mean HFIAS	Mean HDDS	Mean MAHFP	Mean LPI
1	9.2	5.1	10.9	1.15
2	11.0	5.3	10.4	1.36
3	8.3	5.8	10.8	1.00
4	4.9	6.6	11.1	0.57
5	2.7	8.0	11.4	0.29

Whether a household has income from formal wage work or not causes the biggest gap in food security (Table 12). Households with formal wage work have a mean HFIAS score of 4.2, an HDDS of 7.1, and an MAHFP of 11.4, as opposed to corresponding scores of 7.5, 5.9, and 10.9 for those without formal wage incomes. Households with income from informal wage work had the highest mean HFIAS score (7.6) and the lowest HDDS (5.8), indicating much worse food security outcomes than households without income from informal wage work. This finding is cause for concern given that informal wage work is the most common type of income (Figure 10). There was virtually no difference between households with or without income from a formal business and there was a slight advantage for households without income from an informal business compared to those with income from an informal business. The picture that emerges is a link between reliance on the informal economy for a household's livelihood and food insecurity.

TABLE 12: Food Security Scores by Source of Income

Household has income from source		Mean HFIAS	Mean HDDS	Mean MAHFP
Formal wage work	Yes	4.2	7.1	11.4
	No	7.5	5.9	10.9
Informal wage work	Yes	7.6	5.8	11.0
	No	6.1	6.5	11.0
Formal business	Yes	6.6	6.5	11.0
	No	6.7	6.2	11.0
Informal business	Yes	7.0	6.1	10.8
	No	6.6	6.2	11.1

6.8. Mzuzu Food Security in Perspective

The food security scores calculated for Mzuzu can be compared with those from similar surveys conducted by AFSUN and HCP. Table 13 shows the Mzuzu scores in relation to findings from previous urban household food security surveys in Malawi and other African countries. As indicated in the table, some of the surveys are city-wide while others are of particular neighbourhoods. The mean HFIAS score is useful here for comparing the different urban areas at different points in time. Unsurprisingly, the AFSUN surveys conducted in Lilongwe's informal settlements have far higher scores (10.3) than the city-wide surveys conducted in Mzuzu, Maputo (Mozambique), and Nairobi (Kenya). Mzuzu's city-wide result (6.7) is only slightly higher than Maputo (6.5) but nearly a full point higher than Nairobi (5.8). The area that had the lowest mean HFIAS score was South Lunzu, the Blantyre neighbourhood selected for the AFSUN baseline survey in 2008. South Lunzu is a peri-urban area with abundant urban agriculture (Mvula and Chiweza, 2013).

In terms of HFIAP, Lilongwe's informal settlements had a large majority (72%) of households classified as severely food insecure (Table 13). The rate was far lower in the peri-urban area of Blantyre (21%), which also had the highest rate of households classified as food secure (34%). The three city-wide surveys had a remarkably similar result in terms of the proportion of food secure (28%-29%) and mildly food insecure (11%-13%) households. Where Mzuzu differed was in the higher proportion of severely food insecure (45%) relative to moderately food insecure (15%) households. The high rate of severe food insecurity is due to the extreme poverty that exists in Malawi. The combination of rising food costs, precarious incomes, and rapid population growth are contributing to the expansion of extreme poverty in Malawi's cities (Chilanga et al., 2017; Manda, 2013).

TABLE 13: Mzuzu Household Food Security Scores in Regional Perspective

		Lilongwe informal settlements 2015 (N=300)	Blantyre peri-urban transitional area 2008 (N=432)	Mzuzu city-wide 2017 (N=910)	Maputo city-wide 2015 (N=2,071)	Nairobi city-wide 2016 (N=1,414)
HFIAS (Mean)		10.3	5.3	6.7	6.5	5.8
HDDS (Mean)		5.8	6.1	6.2	4.1	6.0
MAHFP (Mean)		8.7	10.0	11.0	10.4	10.8
HFIAP	Food secure	3%	34%	28%	29%	29%
	Mildly food insecure	6%	15%	12%	11%	13%
	Moderately food insecure	19%	30%	15%	22%	33%
	Severely food insecure	72%	21%	45%	38%	25%

7. Food System

7.1. Household Food Sources

This section of the report draws attention to where households source their food, focusing on the link in the food chain that directly precedes consumption by households. Many of these sources are places where people purchase food. The Main Market is in the centre of the city at the intersection of roads going north to Tanzania, south to Lilongwe, and east to Nkhata Bay and Lake Malawi. It is occupied by vendors who rent stalls from the city. Vigwagwa Market is about one kilometre north of the Main Market. It evolved informally in the area adjacent to the air strip and is now also managed by the city, although it does not have the permanent structure of the Main Market. The supermarket category included the established chain stores of People's and Metro, and the Shoprite store that opened in 2013 at the same intersection as the Main Market. The Shoprite store has dramatically changed the retail landscape in Mzuzu and Northern Malawi by offering easy access to a variety of products (Msimuko, 2013). There are several other types of food sources in the neighbourhoods, such as informal markets, small shops, kiosks, butchers, and street vendors.

In addition to these places where people purchase food, there are the places inside and outside the city where people produce their own food, gather food, and receive food transfers from other households. The rural-urban linkages that facilitate urban food security, which are well documented in the literature on African urban food systems (Bah et al., 2003; Frayne and Crush, 2018; Tacoli, 2007) are evident in this section and in the following sections on household food production, food transfers, and indigenous foods.

Figure 27 shows the percentage of households accessing food from each source in the past year and the frequency with which each food source is used. Only four sources were used by a majority of households: small shops (84%), Main Market (67%), Vigwagwa Market (57%), and supermarkets (54%). Small shops were not only the most popular food source, they were also the source most likely to be used on a frequent basis: 54% of households were buying food at small shops at least five days per week. The second most popular food source used at least five days per week was street sellers (25%), which surpassed Main Market, Vigwagwa Market, and supermarkets. These three centrally located sources tended to be accessed on a weekly or monthly basis.

FIGURE 27: Household Food Sources by Frequency of Access

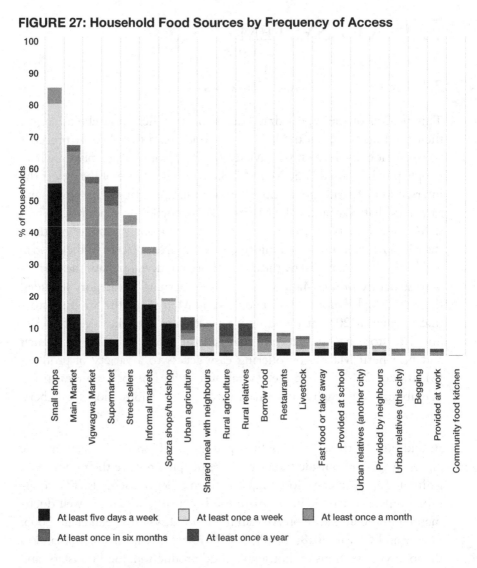

The impact of the food system on the food security status of households is shaped by a myriad cultural and economic factors that go beyond the scope of the survey. However, the cross-tabulation of food source use and food security status reveals some correlations that contribute to the picture of how the food system and food security are linked. Figure 28 compares "food secure" and "food insecure" households' use of the top six food sources. Food secure households were much more likely to use supermarkets than food insecure households (73% compared to 42%). Food secure households were also more likely to use Main Market and Vigwagwa Market. Food insecure households were more likely than food secure households to use small shops, street sellers, and informal markets.

FIGURE 28: Use of Selected Food Sources by Food Security Status

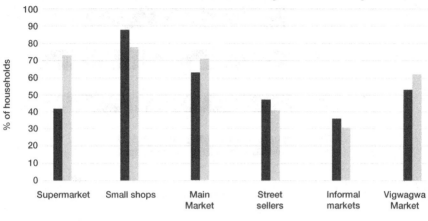

Food insecure (HFIAP severely, moderately food insecure)

Food secure (HFIAP mildly food insecure, food secure)

Supermarkets are fast becoming important sources of food across many cities in the developing world (Crush and Frayne, 2018). They are usually located in convenient areas of cities and their wide range of goods means that customers can get most of the foodstuffs that they need in one location. A total of 38% of Mzuzu households said that they "regularly" shop at a supermarket (as per a separate question from the data in Figure 26). Table 14 provides an analysis of the food security and LPI scores of these two groups of households, showing that the group that regularly shops at supermarkets is far better off on average.

TABLE 14: Food Security and LPI Scores by Supermarket Patronage

	Shops at supermarkets	Does not shop at supermarkets
Mean LPI	0.51	1.04
Mean HFIAS	3.6	8.6
Mean HDDS	7.5	5.4
Mean MAHFP	11.6	10.7
N	344	557

Among the households that normally shop at supermarkets, the main reasons were "supermarkets have a greater variety of foods" (94% in agreement) and "food is better quality at supermarkets" (87%) (Figure 29). The latter could be a reference to concerns about food safety in informal markets and with street vendors. A majority also agreed that they buy in bulk at supermarkets. Among those who do not normally shop at supermarkets, the most common reason was that "supermarkets do not provide credit" (77% in agreement) (Figure 30). About half (49%) agreed that supermarkets are only for the wealthy. The highest rate of disagreement was with the statement, "supermarkets do not sell the food we need" (60%).

FIGURE 29: Reasons for Shopping at Supermarkets

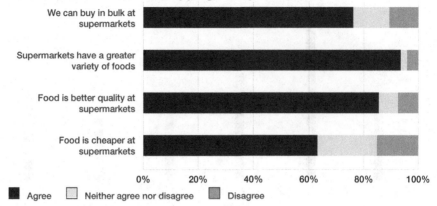

FIGURE 30: Reasons for Not Shopping at Supermarkets

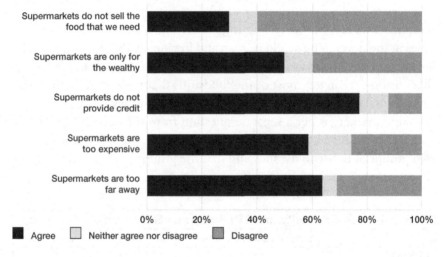

7.2. Food Purchasing Patterns

The Hungry Cities Food Purchases Matrix (HCFPM) contains a standardized list of foods that has been implemented in surveys in large and small cities in various countries in the Global South including in this survey (Crush and McCordic, 2017). It provides an opportunity to compare food purchasing patterns in Mzuzu with other cities. Because the list of foods is being applied internationally, it contains several generic items that were not widely purchased in Mzuzu (e.g. tinned foods, cooked foods, and processed foods). As is indicated below in the section on indigenous foods, the HCFPM also omitted several popular foods in Mzuzu that are not popular elsewhere. The foods that were purchased by most households included sugar (80%), cooking oil (78%), rice (69%), fresh/cooked vegetables (67%), eggs (55%), maize meal (53%), fresh meat (50%), dried fish (50%), and tea/coffee (50%) (Table 15).

TABLE 15: Proportion of Households Purchasing Food Items in the Past Month

Food item (English)	Food item (Chitumbuka)	% of households
Sugar	Shuga	80
Cooking oil	Mafuta ghakuphikira	78
Rice	Mpunga	69
Fresh/cooked vegetables	Mphangwe yambula kuyanika	67
Eggs	Masumbi	55
Maize meal	Ufa	53
Fresh meat	Nyama ya yiwisi	50
Dried fish	Nsomba yakwanika	50
Tea/coffee	Tiyi/khofi	50
Fresh fish	Nsomba yayiwisi (fresh)	47
Fresh fruit	Vipaso vyakupambanapambana	41
Fresh milk	Mukaka wa maji	37
White bread	Buledi mu tuba	34
Frozen chicken	Nkhuku yamufuliji	30
Fresh chicken	Nkhuku ya yiwisi	30
Pasta	Vyakulya ngati supageti, makaloni na vinyakhe vinandi	21
Brown bread	Buledi wa bulauni	15
Snacks	Twakukazinga na twakubeking'a ngati khirisipi, tumasikono	14
Offal	Vyamukati mwa nyama ngati matumbo, na vinyakhe vinandi	10
Sweets/chocolate	Vyakunong'omera ngati/chokoleti	10
Frozen meat	Nyama ya kuzizimitsa mu mufuliji	9
Chips/french fries	Mbambaira/mbatatesi yakukazinga	9
Dried vegetables	Mphangwe yakwanika	7
Frozen fish	Nsomba ya mafuliji	5
Pies/samoosa/vetkoek	Samosa na vinyakhe vinandi	5
Sour milk	Chambiko	5
Cooked meat	Nyama yakuphika	4
Cooked fish	Nsomba yakuphika	4
Cooked chicken	Nkhuku yakuphika	2
Tinned/canned vegetables	Mphangwe iliyose yamuvithini	1
Tinned/canned fruit	Vipaso vyamuvithini	1
Dried fruit	Vipaso vyakunika/kuyanika/kufutsa	1
Tinned/canned meat	Nyama yamuchithini	1
Dried meat	Nyama yakwanika	0

7.2.1. Food Purchases by Source

For each of the items purchased, respondents identified where the household normally purchases that item. The responses for the most widely purchased items are compiled in Figure 31. For the key grocery items of sugar, cooking oil, and tea or coffee, the majority normally purchased them at small shops and about one-third at supermarkets. Fresh or cooked vegetables were mostly purchased from street sellers, although informal and formal markets were also popular sources. Dried fish and fresh fruit were both mostly purchased at formal markets, followed by informal markets and street sellers.

FIGURE 31: Normal Source for Food Purchases

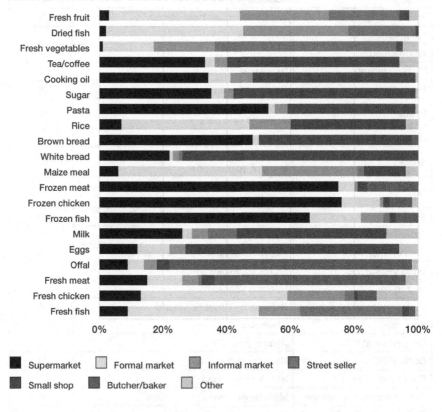

Most households that purchased frozen foods (meat, fish, and chicken) did so at supermarkets (Figure 31). Supermarkets were also the main source of pasta purchases. Brown bread was evenly split between supermarkets and small shops, but white bread was much more likely to be purchased at a small shop (73%) than at a supermarket (22%). Maize meal was most commonly purchased at a formal market (46%), followed by an informal market (30%), and a small shop (13%). There was little consistency in where people normally purchased fresh animal-based products:

fresh fish and chicken were most likely to be purchased at formal markets (Main Market or Vigwagwa Market). A majority of households normally purchased fresh meat at a butchery. Two-thirds of households normally purchased eggs at small shops, which was also the most popular source of milk (47%).

7.2.2. Food Purchases by Location

For each location cited as the normal purchasing source for a particular food, respondents indicated where this source was located geographically. Almost all purchases were normally made within the city. Among the sources located outside of the city, most were located in other urban areas. Notably, this applies to HCFPM food purchases only and not to the indigenous foods and other sources of food from rural areas discussed below. Fresh or cooked vegetables had the highest share purchased "within neighbourhood" (90%), followed by eggs (79%), tea or coffee (70%), and fresh meat, dried fish, and sugar (all with 65%).

7.2.3. Food Purchase Frequency

For each food purchased in the month prior to the survey, the HCFPM collects data on the typical frequency with which the food is purchased. The food purchased most frequently among the top 10 foods in Table 15 was fresh or cooked vegetables: 86% of households purchased them at least five days per week (Figure 32). For all other foods, fewer than 20% purchased them this frequently. Dried fish and fresh fish were both most likely to be purchased on a weekly basis (57% and 55% respectively). The food most likely to be purchased on a monthly basis was rice (50%).

The frequency of purchasing different food items reflects their accessibility. In one sense, higher frequency indicates a consistent supply of a certain food, convenience in accessing it, and a desire for freshness. On the other hand, it can also indicate that people do not have enough money to buy foods in bulk, do not have facilities in the home for storage, and that they live on income sources that fluctuate daily. Figures 32-35 examine the relationship between frequency of purchase and food security status for selected key foods (sugar, cooking oil, dried fish, and maize meal).

Sugar and cooking oil show a consistent pattern with a progression from infrequent purchases among the most food secure households to frequent purchases among the most food insecure households (Figures 33 and 34). For these staples that are easy to store, this pattern reflects the irregular cash flow of many low-income households and suggests a correlation with household food insecurity. Frequent purchases can also mean that households spend more on food and groceries because they are unable to buy in bulk and instead pay marked-up prices to resellers.

FIGURE 32: Popular Food Purchases by Frequency of Purchase

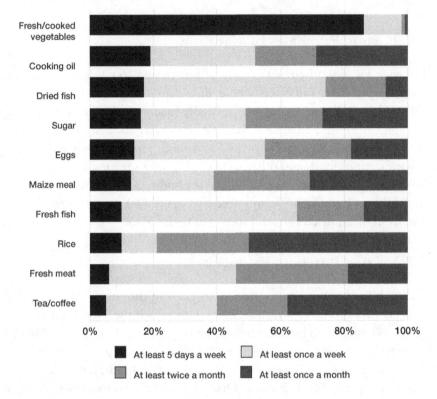

FIGURE 33: Frequency of Purchasing Sugar by Food Security Status

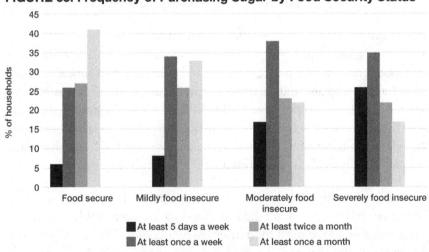

FIGURE 34: Frequency of Purchases of Cooking Oil by Food Security Status

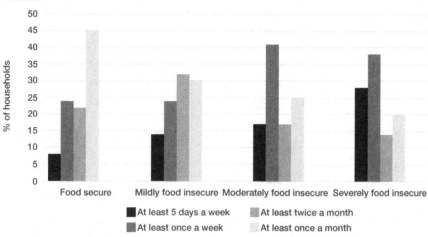

Dried fish does not show the same consistent pattern (Figure 35). Mildly and moderately food insecure households made purchases on a more frequent basis than food secure and severely food insecure households. All food security categories had a similar proportion (55%-59%) of households purchasing dried fish on a weekly basis. Maize meal showed a general trend toward severely food insecure households purchasing it more frequently but the linear relationship was not as clear as with sugar and cooking oil (Figure 36). Food secure households had the second highest percentage of households purchasing at least five times per week (less than severely food insecure but more than mildly and moderately food insecure). Moreover, the severely food insecure households were the most evenly divided in terms of the frequency with which they purchased maize meal.

FIGURE 35: Frequency of Purchases of Dried Fish by Food Security Status

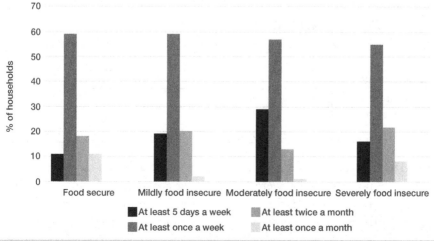

FIGURE 36: Frequency of Purchases of Maize Meal by Food Security Status

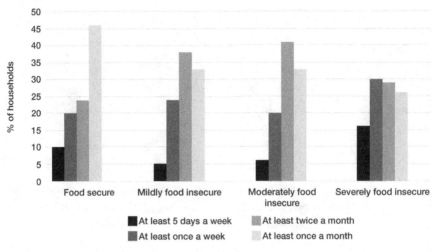

7.3. Household Food Production

7.3.1. Urban Agriculture

Urban agriculture in Sub-Saharan Africa is sometimes seen by development agencies as a panacea to urban food insecurity or poverty (Mougeot, 2005). Researchers have questioned this conclusion's validity, stressing the broad set of labour, land, and financial constraints on poor urban households (Crush et al., 2011). Some 38% of households in Mzuzu said that they grew some of their own food in the city. This figure exceeds the rate in the HCP city-wide survey in Maputo (18%). It also exceeds most low-income urban neighbourhoods in the AFSUN baseline survey (Frayne et al., 2016). Table 16 shows that households that grow food in the city fare marginally better on average than those that do not.

TABLE 16: Urban Agriculture, Food Security and Poverty		
	Grows food in the city	Does not grow food in the city
Mean LPI	0.76	0.88
Mean HFIASS	6.5	6.8
Mean HDDS	6.3	6.2
Mean MAHFP	11.1	11.0
N	340	561

In Mzuzu, urban agriculture is a socially acceptable practice with only 4% of respondents who were not growing any food agreeing with the statement that farming is for rural people only (Figure 37). There appears to be a strong desire to grow food, but people are inhibited by a lack of access to land and inputs. Eighty percent of respondents who do not grow food cited the absence of land as the reason. The inability to access other inputs such as seeds, water, and fertilizer is a barrier for 37%. The desire to farm is evident in that a strong majority (91%) disagreed that they had no interest in growing food and the same proportion disagreed that it was easier to buy food than to grow it.

FIGURE 37: Reasons for Not Engaging in Urban Agriculture

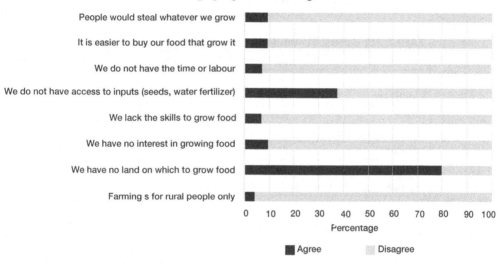

Of those growing food in the city, the largest proportion (42%) were doing so on "other urban land," referring largely to open spaces in the city that they claim for the activity (Table 17). However, 39% were practising urban agriculture on their own housing plots, while 14% were doing so within a residential area outside their own plots. Other less popular locations were on riverbeds, on roadsides, on industrial sites, and with hanging gardens.

TABLE 17: Locations Where People Grow Food in the City			
	No. of households	% of all households	% of households growing food
On own housing plot	232	25	68
Hanging garden	42	5	12
Within residential area, but outside own plot	40	4	11
On riverbed	5	0.5	1
On roadside	4	0.4	1
On industrial site	2	0.2	0.6
Urban forest	0	0	0
Other urban land	39	4	11
Note: Multiple-response question			

The most popular crop was maize, which is grown by a third of all households in Mzuzu and 89% of households growing food crops in the city (Table 18). The next most popular crops were vegetables and beans. Tomatoes and Irish potatoes were produced by fewer than 10% of farming households. The "other" crops category reflected the diversity of crops produced in Mzuzu and included bananas, cabbage, cassava, mangoes, masuku (a local fruit), sugarcane, avocado, groundnuts, guava, tangerines, pawpaw, pumpkin, eggplant, okra, coco yam, sweet potato, rice, peas, onions, pineapple, and soya.

TABLE 18: Crops Grown in Urban Areas

	No. of households	% of all households	% of crop producers
Maize	301	33	89
Vegetables	140	15	41
Beans	93	10	27
Irish potatoes	32	4	9
Tomatoes	25	3	7
Other	48	5	14

Note: Multiple-response question

7.3.2. Urban Livestock

About one in five households kept livestock for food in the city. Of these, 76% kept local chickens (varieties that have tougher meat), 8% kept exotic chickens (these have softer, lighter-coloured meat and are typically used in restaurants and industrial meat production), 10% kept pigeons, 6% kept rabbits, and 1% had cattle (Table 19). Twenty-one percent of households with livestock had "other" livestock, including sheep, pigs, ducks, and goats. Consistent with the findings from the crop-growing component of urban agriculture, the reasons for not participating in livestock rearing centred on access to land and inputs (Figure 38). The willingness to keep livestock and the perceived ability to raise the livestock are similarly high although theft (20%) is of greater concern for livestock than crops (9%).

TABLE 19: Types of Livestock Kept in the City for Food

	No. of households	% of all households	% of livestock owners
Local chicken	149	16	76
Pigeons	19	2	10
Exotic chicken	15	2	8
Rabbits	12	1	6
Cows	2	0.2	1
Other	41	5	21

Note: Multiple-response question

FIGURE 38: Perceptions of Households Not Keeping Livestock in the City

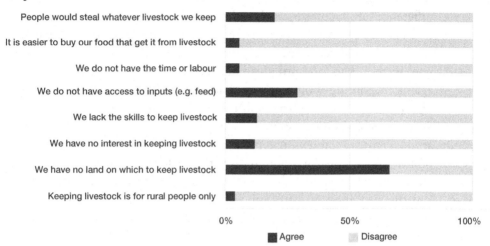

7.3.3. Rural Agriculture

About one in three households in the City of Mzuzu (35%) produce some of the food that they consume on rural farms. Of these, 96% produced maize (Table 20). Cassava was the only other crop with a sizeable share of the rural crop production (15%). Nearly half (48%) of households producing food in rural areas listed other food crops, including one or more of the following: beans, coco yams, soya, avocado, groundnuts, pigeon pea, leafy vegetables (*mphangwe*), sweet potatoes, Irish potatoes, cassava, pumpkins, mangoes, tomatoes, cabbage, sugar cane, and eggplant.

TABLE 20: Crops Grown in Rural Areas

Crop	No. of households	% of all households	% of rural food producers
Maize	303	33	96
Rice	9	1	3
Cassava	47	5	15
Banana	12	1	4
Pineapple	2	0.2	0.6
Other	151	17	48

The mean length of time it takes to reach the place where rural crops are usually produced by the usual means of travel was 12 hours and 41 minutes. However, the mean was skewed by the 12 households that reported that it took 10 hours or more to reach their farms, probably because of the poor transportation networks in northern districts such as Chitipa, or the possibility that these households have farms in Tanzania or Southern Malawi. The median and the mode were only one hour, suggesting that most of these households have rural farms relatively close to Mzuzu.

Households that grow food in the rural areas fare better in terms of food security and LPI than households that do not (Table 21). The margin of difference on all scores is much wider than the comparison between urban farmers and those who do not farm in the city (Table 16). This could suggest a causal relationship whereby the food produced in rural areas goes further than food produced in urban areas in protecting households against becoming food insecure. Alternatively, it could be a reflection of households with higher wealth who can afford to pay for labour and farming inputs, and in some cases land rents, to produce food in rural areas. Figure 39 shows the percentage of households in each income quintile practising rural agriculture: the first, third and fourth quintile are all roughly around 40% but the second quintile is much lower (15%) and the wealthiest group is much higher (61%). The higher income of the households growing food in the rural areas would have improved the mean scores in Table 21.

TABLE 21: Rural Production, Food Security and Poverty

	Grows food in the rural areas	Does not grow food in the rural areas
Mean LPI	0.64	0.94
Mean HFIASS	5.5	7.4
Mean HDDS	6.7	6.0
Mean MAHFP	11.3	10.9
N	315	571

FIGURE 39: Percentage of Households Growing Food in Rural Areas by Income Quintile

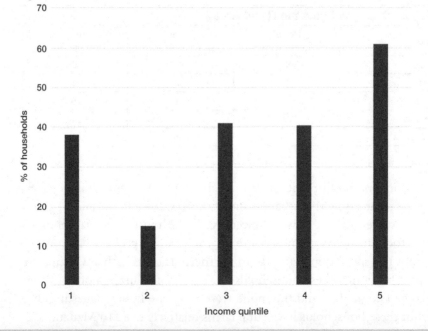

7.4. Food Transfers

Food transfers are an important non-commercial food source for urban households in Southern Africa (Nickanor et al., 2016). The AFSUN baseline survey found that 28% of households in low-income urban areas received transfers, although the percentage ranged from as few as 14% in Johannesburg to as many as 47% in Windhoek, Namibia (Chikanda et al., 2018). The figure for South Lunzu in Blantyre was 35%. The percentage of households receiving transfers in Mzuzu was remarkably the same as the AFSUN baseline average at 28%. These households received food transfers from one or more sources including rural friends, rural relatives, urban friends, and urban relatives. The most common source was rural relatives (20% of all households and 73% of transfer-receiving households) (Table 22). About one in three (34%) transfer-receiving households received transfers from an urban source.

TABLE 22: Households Receiving Food Transfers			
Source	No.	% of all households	% of households receiving transfers
Rural relatives	179	20	73
Rural friends	13	1	5
Urban relatives	46	5	19
Urban friends	50	6	20
No transfers	639	72	–
Note: Multiple-response question			

Maize was the most important food transfer item, received by 81% of recipient households (Table 23). Of the households receiving maize, 80% came from rural areas, and 24% from other urban areas, indicating that some households received maize from both. The rural:urban ratio is similar for rice, although only 7% of recipient households received rice. Fruit and vegetables make up the next most numerous categories, with similar percentages coming from urban sources (74% and 77% respectively) as opposed to rural sources (45% and 32%). The only transfers solely of urban origin were sugar and salt.

Most maize transfers occur at least once per year (64% of households), with 36% receiving transfers more than three times per year. Almost all deem these transfers important to the household (Figure 40). Further studies could delineate the approximate amount of maize and other transfers that are provided per transfer to understand if this is a factor in the perceived importance of the transfers.

TABLE 23: Types of Food Transferred and Geographical Source

Food item	% of recipient households	Rural origin (% of recipient households from this source)	Urban origin (% of recipient households from this source)
Maize	81	80	24
Vegetables	19	32	77
Fruit	13	45	74
Cassava	10	71	33
Sweet potato	9	41	59
Rice	7	82	24
Salt	6	0	100
Sugar	5	0	100
Fish	4	44	56
Meat	2	33	67
Tinned food	0	–	–

Note: Multiple-response question

FIGURE 40: Importance of Food Transfers among Transfer-Receiving Households

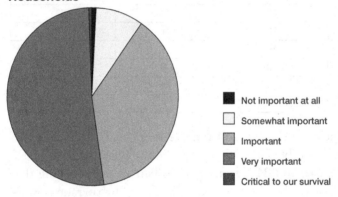

- Not important at all
- Somewhat important
- Important
- Very important
- Critical to our survival

7.5. Indigenous Foods

Especially in secondary cities, the food system relies on a host of foods unique to each city's environment and cultural traditions. To fully capture the indigenous foods consumed in each city, the survey included a set of questions pertaining to the consumption of a list of indigenous foods compiled with the local research team. The aim was to capture a variety of foods in terms of nutritional significance, to highlight foods that are popular locally, and to focus on foods that occur naturally in the local environment. Although no guarantees can be made as to the "indigeneity" of all of these foods, we employ the term as a heuristic device to produce data in response to broader debates about "wild foods" (Mollee et al., 2017; Sneyd, 2013; Van Vliet and Mbazza, 2011), the colonial nature of urban consumption patterns (Riley and Dodson, 2017; De Groote and

Kimenju, 2008), the ecological case for diversification of agriculture and diets (Bezner Kerr, 2014), and the rich diversity of African cuisines that are threatened by the homogenization of urban diets (Noack and Pouw, 2015).

The most widely consumed indigenous foods in the year prior to the survey, consumed by a majority of households, were mushrooms (67%), *therere* (64%), *bondwe* (57%), *mapeyala* (56%), and *masuku* (55%) (Figure 41). *Bondwe* was the most frequently consumed (37% at least once per week), followed by *mapeyala* (22%). In terms of animal and insect-based foods, *mphalata* (41%) was the most popular food. Only 7% of households had consumed bushmeat in the year before the survey, although 8% of consumers consumed it on a weekly basis suggesting that it is consistently available in Mzuzu.

FIGURE 41: Frequency of Consumption of Indigenous Foods

y-axis: % of households (0 to 100)

Categories (x-axis): Nkhlowani (Mushrooms), Therere (okra greens), Bondwe (amaranth), Mapeyala (tamarind), Masuku (fruit), Mphalata (flying ants), Malambe (baobab fruit), Masimbi (coco yam), Uchi (honey), Chinaka (yam), Chilazi (yam), Bushmeat, Tiyuni (small birds), Dongo (edible clay), Mpoza (fruit), Mathyokolo (fruit), Nkhungu (lakefly), Mphalabungu (caterpillar)

Legend:
- At least once a week
- At least once a month
- At least 3-6 times per year
- At least once a year

Table 24 supplements the preceding sections by providing information about where households access indigenous foods. It reveals more of the wide range of food sources in and beyond the city and the central importance of urban–rural linkages for households in Mzuzu. The dominant means of accessing these foods is through purchase at an urban market or street vendor (Table 24). The only indigenous food that is accessed in any quantity at a supermarket is honey (26%), which reflects the fact that it is not exclusively sold through local distribution channels. Several households also collect honey from rural (7%) and urban areas (6%) or have it sent from a rural area (4%). *Mathyokolo*, a local fruit, is the food that is most likely to be collected in a rural area (33%) and *bondwe* is the food most often collected in the city (25%).

For each indigenous food consumed, the respondent was asked to agree or disagree with six possible reasons for consumption. Table 25 shows the average number agreeing with each reason for each food (e.g. if 10% of households consuming mushrooms agreed it was for nutritious reasons, and 20% of households consuming tamarind agreed it was for nutritious reasons, the average would be 15% for nutritious reasons regardless of the proportional popularity of these foods). It also identifies the foods with the highest level of agreement for each reason for consumption. Conclusions about the overall reasons people are consuming indigenous foods should be drawn with caution but there are some striking trends. Few people said that any of the foods were consumed for "cultural or ceremonial reasons." The reason most often agreed with was "nutrition or health reason," which could have several meanings but suggests a practical rather than a cultural reason for consuming these kinds of foods.

People consume indigenous foods for a variety of reasons and it is problematic to assume that they are a last resort when other food is unavailable. A key question embedded in the survey was therefore whether people consume indigenous foods because they cannot afford other foods or because they choose to consume them regardless of resource constraints. The difference in the average percentage agreeing that a food was part of a meal when they had or did not have money to buy food was slight (11% and 13% respectively) (Table 25). This suggests that, in general, indigenous food consumption is not motivated by resource constraints. However, despite the overall low average percentage for eating indigenous foods when money was tight, specific foods elicited a higher percentage. *Bondwe*, *chilazi*, and *therere* grow wild in the city and can therefore be consumed when there is no money to buy food. Also of note is the high percentage of households consuming bushmeat when they have money to buy food (24%), a finding that resonates with the literature showing that bushmeat is a luxury item in urban Africa (Bachand et al., 2015).

TABLE 24: Sources for Purchases of Indigenous Foods

Food item (English/ Chitumbuka)	Super-market	Small shop	Market in the city	Market in the coun-tryside	Street seller/ trader	Grown in city	Col-lected in city	Grown in rural area	Col-lected in rural area	Sent from rural area	Other
Vegetables (% of households accessing each food at each source)											
Therere (okra greens)	–	1	49	10	44	6	11	2	5	1	4
Bondwe (amaranth)	–	–	42	9	36	21	25	4	6	2	2
Masimbi (coco yam)	1	3	72	16	21	7	6	4	6	3	2
Chilazi (yam)	–	–	51	4	39	0	1	4	6	4	6
Chinaka (yam)	–	–	66	12	28	2	3	1	6	3	3
Fruits (% of households accessing each food at each source)											
Malambe (baobab fruit)	1	7	72	13	21	0	4	–	2	1	2
Masuku (fruit)	–	–	50	14	37	4	18	4	9	6	2
Mpoza (fruit)	–	–	48	14	23	2	5	2	16	11	2
Mathyokolo (fruit)	5	–	26	19	14	2	5	5	33	16	5
Meats (% of households accessing each food at each source)											
Tiyuni (small birds)	3	–	15	19	32	2	12	–	12	3	12
Bushmeat	3	–	16	18	36	–	5	–	11	16	8
Insects (% of households accessing each food at each source)											
Mphalata (flying ants)	–	–	56	9	36	1	17	–	5	2	4
Nkhungu (lakefly)	6	–	32	10	23	3	3	–	19	13	3
Mphalabungu (caterpillar)	5	–	20	20	40	0	5	5	20	15	–
Other (% of households accessing each food at each source)											
Nkhowani (mushrooms)	1	–	44	8	39	1	14	1	9	4	4
Uchi (honey)	29	13	41	10	16	1	6	–	7	4	4
Mapeyala (tamarind)	1	2	49	11	29	20	15	2	3	1	5
Dongo (edible clay)	–	12	50	4	21	2	10	–	–	4	10

Note: Multiple-response question

TABLE 25: Reasons for Consuming Indigenous Foods

Reason for consuming	Average percentage agreeing with reason for consuming each food	Top foods consumed for reason
Part of meal when you have money to buy food	11%	Masimbi (coco yam) (26%) Bushmeat (24%) Nkhowani (mushroom) (16%)
Part of meal when you don't have money to buy food	13%	Bondwe (amaranth) (37%) Chilazi (yam) (30%) Therere (okra greens) (29%)
A snack between meals	22%	Masuku (fruit) (50%) Chinaka (yam) (46%) Mpoza (fruit) and Mapeyala (tamarind) (tied at 43%)
Nutrition or health reasons	45%	Uchi (honey) (73%) Bondwe (amaranth) (68%) Tiyuni (small birds) (64%)
Cultural or ceremonial reasons	5%	Mphalabungu (caterpillar) (15%) Nkhungu (lakefly) (10%) Chinaka (yam) (8%)
Gift	10%	Bushmeat (29%) Malambe (baobab fruit) (29%) Nkhungu (lakefly) (19%)
Other	27%	Dongo (edible clay) (68%) Mphalata (flying ants) (44%) Therere (okra greens) (41%)

There were high rates of citation of "other" reasons for consuming these foods. Most of the recorded responses related to taste preferences and because they were used to consuming these foods. The items with the highest rates of response here were *dongo* (68%), *mphalata* (44%) and *therere* (41%). The top reasons for eating *dongo* were for pleasure, to reduce nausea, because of pregnancy (perhaps overlapping with the "nausea" reason), as a luxury, and because of an addiction to eating it. The top reasons for *mphalata* were that people "just liked eating it" or that it was a normal meal. Some people said that it was a luxury and others said that it was something children liked, something they eat when it is in season, and that they eat it when it is the only food available. For *therere*, the vast majority also said it was a preferred food or just a normal food to eat. A few respondents said "for variety's sake" and one felt "like eating okra with the belief that it is part of the six food groups."

8. CONCLUSION

This report has provided details about the demographic characteristics of the population of the City of Mzuzu, their food security experiences, and their interaction with the food system. Key findings include:

- Mzuzu has a very youthful population: half of the population is under the age of 20 and one-quarter is under the age of 10;

- One-quarter live in a house with an indoor kitchen and bathroom and the majority do not have these amenities inside their homes;

- In the year prior to the survey, three-quarters of the households experienced interruptions in electricity and one-third "always" went without electricity;

- In the month prior to the survey, 62% of households worried about not having enough food and 27% had gone a whole day and night without eating anything because they did not have the resources to access food;

- 45% of households were severely food insecure;

- The mean Household Dietary Diversity Score was 6.2 out of 12;

- Households in which the head was older, female, and unmarried were the most food insecure;

- Households that had an income from a formal wage were more food secure than households in which no one earned a formal wage;

- Small shops were the most popular food source, followed by the two formal markets (Main Market and Vigwagwa Market), supermarkets, and street vendors;

- Food secure households were more likely to use supermarkets and, correspondingly, households that used supermarkets were more food secure;

- 38% of households produced some of their own food in the city and they were slightly more food secure than households that did not produce any food in the city;

- 35% of households produced food on a rural farm and they were much more food secure than households that did not produce any food in the rural areas; and

- Most households consumed some indigenous foods, which they usually accessed at city markets or from street traders.

The research proves that food insecurity is an urgent issue and a serious problem for many households in Mzuzu. The most vulnerable households are those without a formal wage income, households headed by older people, especially older women, and households that are not able to produce food in the rural areas. The research also shows that the food system is dynamic and diverse, with households accessing food from a variety of formal and informal food sources and relying on rural-urban linkages for urban survival. Urban and rural agriculture are important features of the food system, but there is little evidence that these are the "self-help" responses to poverty that urban agriculture advocates in Africa sometimes imply. The same can be said of the importance of food transfers, which bolster food security by social linkages within and outside of the city.

This report marks the beginning of a series of conversations with policy-makers, community leaders, and residents in Mzuzu and other secondary cities about the nature of urban food security and how to promote household food security in tandem with efforts to reduce poverty, enhance inclusiveness, improve public health, and ensure ecological sustainability as the cities grow. Some general observations that can help to guide these conversations and inspire future research are:

- Identifying the underlying causes of vulnerability for identified groups (e.g. widows, senior citizens, people working in the informal economy, people without land) and drawing attention to ways of offering systematic support to these groups;

- Addressing youth unemployment as a key factor in household food insecurity;

- Identifying the multiple actors within the informal food systems, including the production and marketing of indigenous foods, the social linkages that facilitate household food production and food transfer, and the management of informal markets, in order to strengthen these systems that serve as a critically important supplement to the formal food system; and

- Promoting dietary diversity by influencing people to choose indigenous and locally produced foods. This will involve public awareness campaigns and measures to ensure the safety of these foods.

ENDNOTE

1.   Exchange rate calculated at USD 0.0014 = 1 MWK based on historical conversion rates available at: http://www.xe.com/currencytables/?from=MWK&date=2017-02-24

REFERENCES

1. Aberman, N., Meerman, J. and Benson, T. (eds.) (2015). *Mapping the Linkages Between Agriculture, Food Security and Nutrition in Malawi* (Washington, DC: IFPRI).

2. Afrobarometer (2004). *Lived Poverty in Africa: Desperation, Hope and Patience.* Afrobarometer Briefing Paper No. 11, Cape Town.

3. Bachand, N., Arsenault, J., and Ravel, A. (2015). "Urban Household Meat Consumption Patterns in Gabon, Central Africa, With a Focus on Bushmeat" *Human Dimensions of Wildlife* 20: 147-158.

4. Bah, M., Cissé, S., Diyamett, B., Diallo, G., Lerise, F., Okali, D., Okpara, E., Olawoye, J., and Tacoli, C. (2003). "Changing Rural-Urban Linkages in Mali, Nigeria and Tanzania" *Environment & Urbanization* 15: 13-23.

5. Battersby, J. (2017). "MDGs to SDGs – New Goals, Same Gaps: The Continued Absence of Urban Food Security in the Post-2015 Global Development Agenda" *African Geographical Review* 36: 115-129.

6. Bezner Kerr, R. (2014). "Lost and Found Crops: Agrobiodiversity, Indigenous Knowledge, and a Feminist Political Ecology of Sorghum and Finger Millet in Northern Malawi" *Annals of the Association of American Geographers* 104: 577-593.

7. Bilinsky, P. and Swindale, A. (2007). *Months of Adequate Household Food Provisioning (MAHFP) for Measurement of Household Food Access: Indicator Guide* (Washington, DC: Academy for Educational Development).

8. Chikanda, A., Crush, J., and Frayne, B. (2018). "Migration and Urbanization: Consequences for Food Security" In B. Frayne, J. Crush, and C. McCordic (eds.), *Food and Nutrition Security in Southern African Cities* (New York: Routledge), pp. 48-65.

9. Chilanga, E., Riley, L., Ngwira, J., Chalinda, C. and Masitala, L. (2017). *The State of Food Insecurity in Lilongwe's Informal Settlements, Malawi.* AFSUN Report No. 26, Cape Town.

10. Chilowa, W. (1991). "Food Insecurity and Coping Strategies among the Low Income Urban Households in Malawi" Chr. Michelson Institute Report No. 4, Bergen.

11. Coates, J., Swindale, A. and Bilinsky, P. (2007). *Household Food Insecurity Access Scale (HFIAS) for Measurement of Household Food Access: Indicator Guide (Version 3). Food and Nutrition Technical Assistance Project* (Washington, DC: Academy for Educational Development).

12. Crush, J. and Frayne, B. (2018). "The 'Supermarketization' of Food Supply and Retail: Private Sector Interests and Household Food Security" In B. Frayne, J. Crush, and C. McCordic (eds.), *Food and Nutrition Security in Southern African Cities* (New York: Routledge), pp. 168-197.

13. Crush, J., Hovorka, A. and Tevera, D. (2011). "Food Security in Southern African Cities: The Place of Urban Agriculture" *Progress in Development Studies* 11, 285-305.

14. Crush, J. and McCordic, C. (2017). "The Hungry Cities Food Purchases Matrix: A Measure of Urban Household Food Security and Food System Interactions" HCP Discussion Paper No. 10, Waterloo and Cape Town.

15. Crush, J. and Riley, L. (2017). "Urban Food Security and Rural Bias" HCP Discussion Paper No. 11, Waterloo and Cape Town.

58   AFRICAN FOOD SECURITY URBAN NETWORK (AFSUN)

16.   De Groote, H. and Kimenju, S.C. (2008). "Comparing Consumer Preferences for Color and Nutritional Quality in Maize: Application of a Semi-Doublebound Logistic Model on Urban Consumers in Kenya" *Food Policy* 33: 362–370.

17.   Dodson, B., Chiweza, A., and Riley, L. (2012). *Gender and Food Insecurity in Southern African Cities*. AFSUN Report No. 10, Cape Town.

18.   Frayne, B. and Crush, J. (2018). "Food Supply and Urban-Rural Links in Southern African Cities" In B. Frayne, J. Crush, and C. McCordic (eds.), *Food and Nutrition Security in Southern African Cities* (New York: Routledge), pp. 34–47.

19.   Frayne, B., Crush, J., and McCordic, C. (eds.) (2018). *Food and Nutrition Security in Southern African Cities* (New York: Routledge).

20.   Frayne, B., McCordic, C., and Shilomboleni, H. (2016). "The Mythology of Urban Agriculture" In J. Crush and J. Battersby (eds.), *Rapid Urbanisation, Urban Food Deserts and Food Security in Africa* (New York: Springer), pp. 19–32.

21.   Frayne, B. et al. (2010). *The State of Urban Food Insecurity in Southern Africa*. AFSUN Report No. 2, Cape Town.

22.   Gondwe, J. and Ayenagbo, K. (2013). "Negotiating for Livelihoods Beyond the Formal Mzuzu City, Malawi, by the Urban Poor: Informal Settlements as Spaces of Income Generating Activities" *International Journal of Human Sciences* 10: 356–375.

23.   Government of Malawi. National Statistics Office (2016). *Statistical Yearbook* (Zomba: NSO).

24.   Kadzamira, E. and Rose, P. (2001). "Educational Policy Choice and Policy Practice in Malawi: Dilemmas and Disjunctures" IDS Working Paper 124, Brighton.

25.   Kamwendo, G. (2004). "'Your Chitumbuka is Shallow. It's Not the Real Chitumbuka': Linguistic Purism among Chitumbuka Speakers in Malawi" *Nordic Journal of African Studies* 13: 275–288.

26.   Kita, S. (2017). "Urban Vulnerability, Disaster Risk Reduction and Resettlement in Mzuzu City, Malawi" *International Journal of Disaster Risk Reduction* 22: 158–166.

27.   Legwegoh, A. and Riley, L. (2014). "Food, Place, and Culture in Urban Africa: Comparative Consumption in Gaborone and Blantyre" *Journal of Hunger and Environmental Nutrition* 9: 256–279.

28.   Manda, M. (2013). *Situation of Urbanisation in Malawi Report* (Lilongwe: Government of Malawi Ministry of Lands and Housing).

29.   Mambo, S. and Malombe, E. (2014). *Comparative Study of Construction Cost between Firewood Burnt Bricks and Cement Soil Stabilized Blocks for Sustainable Development in Mzuzu City in Malawi*. Unpublished manuscript.

30.   McCracken, J. (2012). *A History of Malawi, 1859-1966* (Woodbridge, UK: James Currey).

31.   Mollee, E., Pouliot, M., and McDonald, M. (2017). "Into the Urban Wild: Collection of Wild Urban Plants for Food and Medicine in Kampala, Uganda" *Land Use Policy* 63: 67–77.

32.   Mougeot, L. (ed.) (2005). *Agropolis: The Social, Political and Environmental Dimensions of Urban Agriculture* (Ottawa: IDRC).

33.   Msimuko, C. (2013, 16 November). "The 10-Million Dollar Mzuzu Shoprite Complex Opens" *Pamtengo News*. Available at http://pamtengo.com/the-10-million-dollar-mzuzu-shoprite-complex-opens/.

34. Mvula, P. and Chiweza, A. (2013). *The State of Food Insecurity in Blantyre City, Malawi.* AFSUN Report No. 18, Cape Town.

35. Nickanor, N., Crush, J. and Pendleton, W. (2016). "Migration, Rural-Urban Linkages and Food Insecurity" In J. Crush and J. Battersby (eds.), *Rapid Urbanisation, Urban Food Deserts and Food Security in Africa* (New York: Springer), pp. 19-32.

36. Noack, A. and Pouw, N (2015) "A Blind Spot in Food and Nutrition Security: Where Culture and Social Change Shape the Local Food Plate" *Agriculture and Human Values* 32: 169-182.

37. Riley, L. (2014). "Operation Dongosolo and the Geographies of Urban Poverty in Malawi" *Journal of Southern African Studies* 40: 443-458.

38. Riley, L. and Dodson, B. (2017). "Intersectional Identities: Food, Space and Gender in Urban Malawi" *Agenda: Empowering Women for Gender Equity* 30: 53-61.

39. Riley, L. and Dodson, B. (2016). "'Gender Hates Men': Untangling Gender and Development Discourses in Food Security Fieldwork in Urban Malawi" *Gender, Place and Culture: A Journal of Feminist Geography* 23: 1047-1060.

40. Riley, L. and Legwegoh, A. (2018). "Gender and Food Security: Household Dynamics and Outcomes. In B. Frayne, J. Crush, and C. McCordic (eds.), *Food and Nutrition Security in Southern African Cities* (New York: Routledge), pp. 86-100.

41. Riley, L. and Legwegoh, A. (2014). "Comparative Urban Food Geographies in Blantyre and Gaborone" *African Geographical Review* 33: 52-66.

42. Roberts, B. (2014). *Managing Systems of Secondary Cities: Policy Responses in International Development* (Brussels: Cities Alliance).

43. Rose, R. (1998). "Getting Things Done With Social Capital: New Russia Barometer VII" Centre for the Study of Public Policy Series No. 303, Glasgow.

44. Satterthwaite, D. (2006). *Outside the Large Cities: The Demographic Importance of Small Urban Centres and Large Villages in Africa, Asia and Latin America* (London: IIED).

45. Sneyd, L. (2013). "Wild Food, Prices, Diets and Development: Sustainability and Food Security in Urban Cameroon" *Sustainability* 5: 4728-4759.

46. Swindale, A and Bilinsky, P. (2006). *Household Dietary Diversity Score (HDDS) for Measurement of Household Food Access: Indicator Guide (Version 2)* (Washington, DC: Academy for Educational Development).

47. Tacoli, C. (2007). "Poverty, Inequality and the Underestimation of Rural-Urban Linkages" *Development* 50: 90-95.

48. Tawodzera, G., Riley, L. and Crush, J. (2016). "Following the Crisis: Poverty and Food Security in Harare, Zimbabwe" *Journal of Food and Nutritional Disorders* 5.

49. UNHABITAT (2011a). *Malawi: Mzuzu Urban Profile.* Nairobi: UNHABITAT.

50. UNHABITAT (2011b). *Malawi: Lilongwe Urban Profile.* Nairobi: UNHABITAT.

51. University of Malawi. Centre for Language Studies (2006). *Language Mapping Survey for Northern Malawi.*

52. Van Vliet, N. and Mbazza, P. (2011). "Recognizing the Multiple Reasons for Bushmeat Consumption in Urban Areas: A Necessary Step Toward the Sustainable Use of Wildlife for Food in Central Africa" *Human Dimensions of Wildlife* 16: 45-54.

53. Vaughan, M. (1987). *The Story of an African Famine: Gender and Famine in Twentieth-Century Malawi* (Cambridge: Cambridge University Press).

54. Williams, S. (1969). "The Beginnings of Mzuzu with Some Biographical Notes of Some Vipya Tung Project Managers" *The Society of Malawi Journal* 22: 46-50.

55. World Bank (2018). *National Accounts Data,* Malawi. Available at https://data.worldbank.org/indicator/NY.GDP.PCAP.CD?locations=MW

Printed in the United States
By Bookmasters